# there's rice at home

**RENE SUBASH**

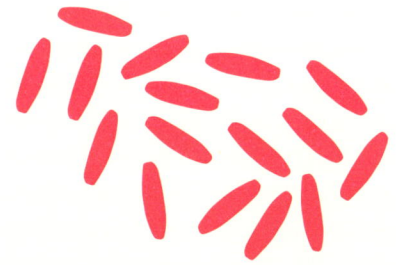

# there's rice at home

**RENE SUBASH**

**80 GLOBAL RECIPES CELEBRATING RICE**

Photography by Haarala Hamilton

Quadrille

# contents

| | |
|---|---|
| introduction | 6 |
| rice 101 | 8 |
| | |
| snacks and small plates | 12 |
| simple weekday meals | 44 |
| weekend cooking | 88 |
| perfect sides | 132 |
| sweet endings | 156 |
| | |
| index | 182 |
| about the author | 188 |
| acknowledgements | 191 |

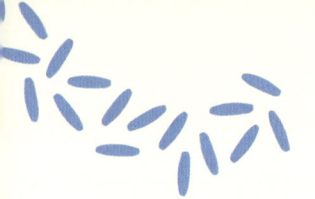

# introduction

'There's rice at home,' is a phrase I heard throughout my childhood in Bangalore, India. And nothing changed when my family moved to the UK – I remember being in the car and begging my parents to stop at a McDonald's on the way home, already knowing what the answer would be: 'No, Rene; there's rice at home'. In Kerala, where my family is from, we have an annual festival called Onam, which celebrates the first rice harvest, so I guess you could say that my love for rice has truly been instilled in my roots.

My earliest memories of cooking were being tasked to help my mum peel and chop onions, ginger and garlic, when I was as young as eight. Over the years, she slowly let me progress to helping to stir and sauté, and eventually I learned how to make entire dishes on my own.

My love for cooking is not just for the food itself, it's for the fact that food brings people together. Every celebration in our family, whether it's a birthday, Easter or Christmas, is always based around the question, 'What should we make?' I genuinely believe that food is at the heart of every memorable gathering and celebration. Seeing people enjoy the dishes that I make brings me so much joy. People say that cooking is a selfless act, but sometimes I think it is a little selfish, purely because of how happy it makes me.

Coming from an Indian background, like most Asian kids I was never encouraged to take up my passion of cooking seriously. It was always 'become a healthcare professional, or a lawyer or an engineer'. And, like a good Indian kid, I listened and studied nursing at university. However, after graduating and starting to work as a nurse at the very peak of the Covid pandemic, I didn't give up on my love for food. I started a TikTok and Instagram page, naming it @Renes. Cravings because I just wanted to share things I was craving (ha-ha) and began using the page as a creative outlet. My job at the time was very stressful. I shared lighthearted videos of my cooking adventures, which helped me relax and feel less anxious and somehow people seemed to like them.

Nursing was becoming increasingly hard for me. The lack of support and poor staffing levels began to negatively impact my mental health, so I ended up going to Spain for my first-ever solo trip. This trip changed my life. I connected with people from all over the world and the one thing everyone connects over is good food!

The trip fuelled my love for travel and experiencing food from all over the world. Since then, I have travelled across Europe, Mexico, Vietnam and South Korea, learning about their foods and cultures, and seeing how it brings everyone together regardless of what language is spoken.

One thing I have found interesting is how nearly every culture has their own version of a rice dish and how rice is used so differently around the world. It's a cupboard staple for a reason! Did you know that rice is one of the most widely consumed grains in the world? More than 50% of the world's population depends on and enjoys rice for 80% of their food requirements. Rice is adaptable and easy to grow, which is why it's grown in every continent (except Antarctica!).

When eating rice and beans in Mexico or bibimbap in South Korea, every bite reminded me of home in some way. That is why I'm so excited to show you all of my favourite ways of cooking with rice. Some people dread cooking it, but once you get the hang of it, you will realize rice is actually one of the most versatile ingredients in the kitchen. You can make tasty snacks, hearty mains and even delicious desserts – all from this one simple grain!

So, if you're looking for tasty, easy and comforting recipes to showcase the bag of rice that you have in the back of your cupboard, be it basmati, long-grain, short-grain or microwave rice, this book will help you turn it into a winner. The book has been split into five simple chapters to help you find the perfect rice recipe, so whether you're looking for a quick rice-fuelled snack, a no-fuss midweek dinner or a hearty feast, a tasty side dish or even a dessert, this book has all the inspo you need.

And always remember our family motto: *There's rice at home!*

Love,

**Rene x**

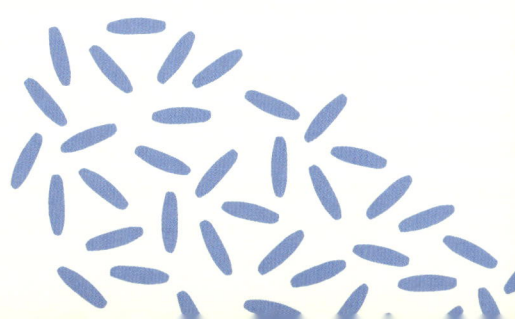

# rice 101

## types of rice

**Long-grain rice:** Their length is up to 3-4 times their width. When cooked, the rice should be fluffy and not very clumpy. The most popular varieties are basmati and jasmine rice.

**Medium-grain rice:** As you might expect, this falls somewhere in between long-grain and short-grain rice. When cooked, medium-grain rice should be moist and fluffy, but after cooling it should slightly harden and clump together. The most popular varieties are arborio and bomba.

**Short-grain rice:** This is sometimes referred to as glutinous or sticky rice, due to its starchy texture. The grains are rounded and stick together in clumps when cooked. Japanese short-grain rice (sushi rice) is one of the popular rices in this category.

**Ready-cooked:** Another thing that is really popular nowadays is microwave rice, which is rice that has already been cooked and packaged. All you have to do is heat it up according to the packet instructions, usually in a microwave or in a pan of boiling water, and you're good to go in just a couple of minutes. I think these are perfect if you're in a rush and just need some rice really quickly.

I love to keep some in my cupboard for those evenings that are super-busy. They work well as a side or even to make some desserts or fried rice. Just make sure you check the packet instructions, as sometimes the rice can just be parboiled and may require further cooking.

## cooking tips

When it comes to cooking rice, there are many different methods. My favourite ways are to use a rice cooker for short-grain rice and a pan on the hob (stove) for long-grain rice. This is purely because I have perfected cooking long-grain rice on the hob, as it's something that is commonly used in my house. I don't cook short-grain rice as often, so using a rice cooker ensures it comes out perfectly every time. Rice can also be pressure-cooked or steamed. You can even cook it 'like pasta'. I know you might think that's crazy, but hear me out! Many parts of India have been using this method for ages. Simply add your rice to boiling water, then drain off the water when it's cooked and you're left with perfectly cooked fluffy rice! For a foolproof way to cook long-grain white rice, my No-Fail White Rice recipe is on page 134. However, if you prefer sushi rice or brown rice, here are some tips:

For the perfect **sushi rice** (serves 2) the golden ratio I like to use is 1 part sushi rice to 1¼ parts water.

**Step 1:** Measure out 190g (1 cup) of raw sushi rice and wash this 3-4 times or until the water drains clear.

**Step 2:** Add the washed and drained sushi rice to a saucepan and add 295ml (1¼ cup) of water and let this soak for 15 minutes.

**Step 3:** Place the pan over a medium heat, bring this to a boil, cover and turn the heat to low and let this cook for 10-12 minutes.

**Step 4:** Once the time is up and you can see that all the water has been absorbed, turn the heat off and allow to steam, covered, for another 10 minutes.

**Step 5:** Fluff up the rice using a rice paddle or rubber spatula (this helps to prevent the grains of rice from breaking) and enjoy.

For the perfect **brown rice** (serves 2) the golden ratio I like to use is 1 part brown rice to 2 parts water.

**Step 1:** Measure out 190g (1 cup) of raw brown rice, place it in a fine sieve (strainer) and rinse it under running cold water at least 3-4 times, or until the water starts to run clear.

**Step 2:** Add the rinsed rice to a pan, add 455ml (2 cups) water and bring to the boil over a high heat.

**Step 3:** When it comes to the boil, cover with a lid and let it simmer on the lowest heat for 30-35 minutes.

**Step 4:** Turn the heat off and leave it covered for a further 10 minutes.

**Step 5:** Fluff the rice up using a rice paddle or rubber spatula (this helps to prevent the grains of rice from breaking) and enjoy!

## storage

To store rice, you must let it cool down once it's been cooked. I spread out the hot cooked rice over a large plate, creating a larger surface area that helps it cool down, and leave it for an hour or two. I then transfer it to an airtight container and store it in the refrigerator. Don't store it for longer than three days. Always reheat rice that's been in the fridge thoroughly. You can also store it in single-serving freezer bags. When needed, just take one out and heat up in the microwave.

## beyond rice

Rice doesn't just come in grain form! Some of the recipes in this book use other rice-based products, such as rice noodles, rice paper and rice cakes. I also use rice flour, which comes in two types: regular rice flour, which is made from long-grain rice and I mainly use in savoury dishes, and glutinous rice flour, which is made from short-grain rice. I mostly use glutinous rice flour for desserts, as it's sweeter and starchier.

## spice it up

Let me introduce you to some of my most loved and used spices, seasonings and cupboard must-haves.

## whole spices

Cumin seeds, fennel seeds, coriander seeds, black peppercorns, star anise, cinnamon sticks, cardamom pods, cloves, mustard seeds, bay leaves and curry leaves are always good to have on hand. You can add them to the water while you cook the rice, to curries for extra flavour, or you can even lightly roast the whole spices and grind them yourself in a pestle and mortar or spice grinder, which brings out more of the flavour, creating your own spice mixes, if liked. I recommend having dried chillies on hand too; these can be used whole or even be blended into stews or sauces. Whole spices are best stored in a cool, dark place and will last for ages.

## ground spices

Spice powders are also essential in my kitchen. Ground turmeric, chilli powder (hot and Kashmiri), garlic powder and smoked paprika are always great to keep on hand, as they can be used in many different recipes. Once bought, they will last for at least two months, as long as you store them in airtight containers, away from direct sunlight. A good tip is to buy your spices from local ethnic supermarkets, as they are usually cheaper and you get way more for your money!

### spice mixes

Two spice mixes that I always like to have on hand for cooking are garam masala and Lebanese 7 spice. Other pre-made mixes like jerk spice, Cajun spice and za'atar are great when you quickly want to season up some protein or veggies, and can be found in most supermarkets.

### fresh herbs

Fresh herbs are a really easy way to give your food an extra zing of flavour: some of my favourites are coriander, parsley, mint and dill. Like with dried spices, you'll find you often get much better value at Asian or Middle Eastern grocery stores than for the tiny packets of herbs you can buy at supermarkets!

### other cupboard essentials

Rice is essential, of course, but there are a few other things that I find just make it easier to whip up something out of nothing. Lentils are extremely versatile and make a great source of protein. I also keep ghee in stock, as it adds so much flavour to dishes. A can of coconut milk can be added to curries, soups, rice and so much more. Canned tomatoes and chickpeas are always useful to have on hand, along with some good old plain (all-purpose) flour. Some type of hot sauce is also great to have, as it can be used in marinades or just on top of your morning eggs to add some extra kick.

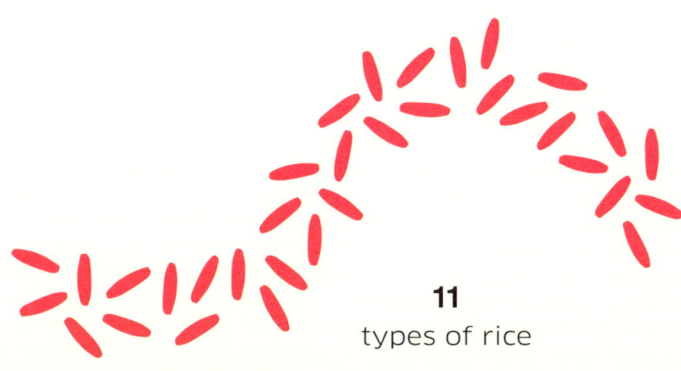

types of rice

# snacks and small plates

When it comes to rice, you might not necessarily think, 'Oh, that would make a great snack.' People usually assume it forms part of a hearty main meal. In this chapter, however, I want to highlight rice in its most snackable, shareable forms. Whether you're rolling it, frying it or shaping it into perfect little balls of happiness, rice is your canvas!

Featuring dishes such as Spicy Tuna Onigiri (page 38), which makes a perfect little midday snack, and Puffed Rice Chaat (page 20) that's spicy, tangy, so so addictive and great for sharing with friends, this chapter is for when you're not quite hungry enough for lunch or dinner and just need a little something to tide you over.

# cheesy arancini balls

**Makes**
6

**Prep Time**
1 hour (plus 4-hour or overnight resting)

1 vegetable stock (bouillon) cube
2 Tbsp olive oil
15g (½oz) unsalted butter
1 white onion, diced
4-5 garlic cloves, minced
190g (1 cup) raw arborio rice
400g (14oz) mushrooms, sliced
10g (¼ cup) chopped fresh parsley
20g (¼ cup) grated Parmesan
sea salt and freshly ground black pepper, to taste

**For the filling and coating**
20g (1oz) cheese, cut into 6 cubes (I like to use mild Cheddar)
35g (¼ cup) plain (all-purpose) flour
1 egg, beaten
40g (½ cup) breadcrumbs
neutral-tasting oil, such as vegetable oil, for deep-frying

Cheesy, crispy arancini are one of my favourite things to make. To speed up this recipe, you could double the quantities for my Mushroom Risotto (page 127) and use the leftovers to make these.

First, make the risotto. In a small saucepan, heat 750ml (3¼ cups) of water and dissolve the stock cube in it. Set aside but keep warm.

In a separate large pan, heat the olive oil and butter over a medium heat, then add the onion and garlic and sauté for 3-4 minutes, or until the onion has softened. Add the rice and sauté for 2-3 minutes, then add the sliced mushrooms and sauté for a further 2-3 minutes.

Add the hot stock, one ladleful at a time, each time stirring until the liquid has evaporated. Once you have added all the stock and the rice is fully cooked, add the parsley and Parmesan, season to taste with salt and pepper, then cover and let the risotto cool fully. This will take at least 4 hours, but overnight is best.

Once the risotto is fully cooled, divide the mixture into 6 and roll each portion into a ball. Use your thumb to make an indent in the middle of each ball, fill with a cube of cheese, then press the rice around the cheese to encase it tightly. Try to cover any gaps, or the cheese may leak out on frying, causing the oil to splatter.

Place the flour, the beaten egg and the breadcrumbs into 3 separate shallow bowls. Dip each ball first into the flour, then into the egg, then into the breadcrumbs until they are all fully coated.

Heat enough oil for deep-frying in a large, deep, heavy-based pan over a medium heat. You will know it is hot enough when a breadcrumb added to the oil sizzles immediately. Deep-fry the balls for 4-5 minutes, or until golden brown.

Remove with a slotted spoon to drain on paper towels and leave to cool for a couple of minutes before serving.

snacks and small plates

# crispy rice bites with imitation crab

**Serves**
4

**Prep Time**
1 hour (plus 2-3 hours freezing)

190g (1 cup) raw sushi rice
1 Tbsp rice vinegar
1 tsp caster (superfine) sugar
neutral-tasting oil, such as vegetable oil, for frying
1 x pack of 16 seafood sticks, finely diced
2 spring onions (scallions), finely sliced
3 Tbsp mayonnaise
2 Tbsp Sriracha sauce

Craving sushi but don't want to break the bank? All the flavours of your favourite sushi roll are in these bite-sized pieces. They're great to make as an appetizer, as the crispy rice contrasts well with the soft texture of the imitation crab.

Wash the rice until the water runs clear. Drain and add the washed rice to a rice cooker along with 350ml (1½ cups) of water. Ideally, the water should be covering the rice to a depth of 2.5cm (1in), so adjust as needed. Cook according to the manufacturer's instructions. If you don't have a rice cooker, feel free to cook in a saucepan following the instructions on page 9.

Once the rice is cooked, mix in the rice vinegar and sugar with a rubber spatula.

Line a 20cm (8in) square baking tin with cling film (plastic wrap) and press the rice into the tin. Place in the freezer for about 2-3 hours until it is firm, but not frozen solid.

Cut the rice block into 16 pieces.

Heat a 2.5cm (1in) depth of oil in a frying pan (skillet) over a medium heat. Fry the pieces on both sides for 4-5 minutes, or until golden brown. Set aside to drain on paper towels.

In a bowl, combine the seafood sticks, spring onions, mayo and Sriracha sauce. Mix well.

snacks and small plates

# veggie rice paper dumplings

**Serves**
2

**Prep Time**
30 minutes

2 Tbsp neutral-tasting oil, such as vegetable oil
2 carrots, shredded
1 tsp grated fresh root ginger
¼ small cabbage, shredded
70g (1 cup) mushrooms, diced
4 garlic cloves, minced
150g (5½oz) firm tofu, crumbled
1 tsp sesame oil
1 Tbsp light soy sauce
3 spring onions (scallions), finely sliced
8 rice paper sheets

**For the dipping sauce**
3 Tbsp light soy sauce
1 tsp Sriracha sauce
1 tsp rice vinegar
1 garlic clove, minced
½ tsp sesame seeds

**Think classic dumplings, just no fiddly wrapping or folding to get the perfect shape!**

Heat 1 tablespoon of the neutral oil in a sauté pan over a medium heat. Add in the carrots, ginger, cabbage, mushrooms, garlic and tofu and sauté for 4-5 minutes.

Add the sesame oil, soy sauce and spring onions and sauté for a further 3-4 minutes.

Remove from the heat and set aside to cool, then divide the mixture into 8 portions.

Take a sheet of rice paper and soak it in a shallow bowl of water for 3-5 seconds until softened. Place it flat on a plate and add one portion of the filling mixture to the centre of the sheet. Fold over the edges, then roll it up so the filling is enclosed.

Repeat until you have used up all the rice paper and filling portions.

Heat the remaining tablespoon of neutral oil in a non-stick frying pan (skillet) over a medium-high heat. Fry the dumplings for 2-3 minutes on each side until crispy.

To make the dipping sauce, mix all of the ingredients together in a bowl and serve alongside the dumplings.

# puffed rice chaat

**Serves**
2

**Prep Time**
20 minutes

½ red onion, finely diced
1 large tomato, finely diced
60g (4 cups) puffed rice
4 Tbsp sev
4 Tbsp roasted peanuts, chopped
4 Tbsp tamarind sauce
2–3 Tbsp shop-bought coriander (cilantro) and mint chutney
2 Tbsp finely chopped fresh coriander (cilantro)
1 tsp chaat masala, or to taste

**This is crispy and packed with spicy, tangy and slightly sweet flavours. Make this for that late afternoon slump when you're not hungry enough for dinner, but peckish enough that you can't stop thinking about what to eat. This is best made as close to the serving time as possible.**

Once you have prepped all of the ingredients, add everything to a bowl and give it a good mix.

Top with an extra sprinkle of chaat masala, if you like, and enjoy!

# spicy rice cake and sausage skewers with gochujang glaze

**Serves**
4

**Prep Time**
30 minutes (plus 30 minutes soaking time)

24 Korean rice cakes (tteok)
2 Tbsp gochujang
2 Tbsp caster (superfine) sugar
1 tsp light soy sauce
½ tsp sesame oil
3 Tbsp hot water
18 mini hot dogs or cocktail sausages
2 Tbsp neutral-tasting oil, such as vegetable oil
1 tsp white sesame seeds

**These sticky, spicy-sweet skewers are a crowd pleaser. The chewy rice cakes and pop of the mini hot dogs make a combination that will leave you wanting more. You will need 6 wooden skewers for this recipe.**

Add the rice cakes to a bowl of hot water and leave to soak for 30 minutes, then drain.

In a bowl, mix together the gochujang, sugar, soy sauce, sesame oil and hot water. Set aside.

Divide the rice cakes and mini hot dogs/sausages into 6 portions and thread alternately onto 6 wooden skewers.

Heat the oil in a frying pan (skillet) over a medium heat. Once hot, fry the skewers on both sides for 5–6 minutes, or until crispy.

Brush both sides of the skewers with the sauce and fry for a further minute on each side.

Sprinkle with sesame seeds and serve.

snacks and small plates

# crispy rice paper crackers

**Serves**
1

**Prep Time**
10 minutes

4 rice paper sheets
neutral-tasting oil, such as vegetable oil, for frying
¼ tsp garlic salt
sweet chilli sauce, to serve

**A great way to use up those sheets of leftover rice paper in your cupboard is to make these rice paper crackers. They're super crispy and light and will leave you reaching for more.**

Use kitchen scissors to cut the rice paper sheets into quarters.

Place a small frying pan (skillet) over a medium-high heat and add enough oil to cover the base of the pan.

When the oil is hot, add the rice paper pieces, one at a time, and watch them puff up. They fry super-quick, so keep an eye on them. Use kitchen tongs to remove them to paper towels to drain. Repeat until they are all fried.

Sprinkle with the garlic salt while they are still hot.

Serve with sweet chilli sauce for dipping.

# crispy rice salad with tahini and lemon

**Serves**
2

**Prep Time**
35 minutes

130g (1 cup) cooked rice of choice
1 tsp sesame oil
1 tsp light soy sauce
80g (½ cup) shelled edamame
½ cucumber, finely sliced
1 avocado, flesh chopped
3 spring onions (scallions), chopped
2 garlic cloves, minced
3 Tbsp roasted peanuts
2 Tbsp finely chopped fresh mint
3 Tbsp olive oil
2 Tbsp tahini
2 Tbsp lemon juice
1½ tsp honey
½ tsp salt
½ tsp freshly ground black pepper

**Sometimes salads can be boring, but not this one! The crispy rice, zesty dressing and extra crunch of the nuts keeps me coming back for more.**

Preheat the oven to 200°C fan/220°C/425°F/Gas mark 7 and line a baking sheet with baking parchment.

In a bowl, mix together the cooked rice, sesame oil and soy sauce.

Spread the rice mixture over the prepared baking sheet and cook in the oven for 15-20 minutes until the rice is brown and very crispy.

Combine the remaining salad ingredients in a large bowl and give them a good mix before adding the crispy rice. Stir and enjoy!

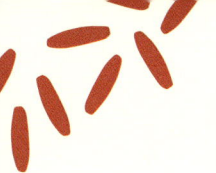

# rice cutlets

**Serves**
2

**Prep Time**
30 minutes

195g (1½ cups) cooked rice
1 tsp ginger and garlic paste
1 small onion, finely diced
2 green chillies, finely chopped
½ tsp cumin seeds
1 tsp Kashmiri chilli powder
¼ tsp garam masala
2 Tbsp chopped fresh coriander (cilantro)
2–3 Tbsp gram flour (besan)
½ tsp salt
neutral-tasting oil, such as vegetable oil, for frying

**We all have times when there's leftover rice in the refrigerator and we're not sure what to do with it. These crispy rice cutlets are something my grandmother used to whip up, because nothing goes to waste in her house! I love serving these with lots of ketchup.**

Place the cooked rice in a bowl and use a potato masher to give it a good mash until some of the rice grains are broken and it starts to get stuck together.

Add all the other ingredients, except the oil, and give everything a mix with your hands. You want the mixture to be able to hold its shape.

Divide the mixture into 6 balls and slightly flatten them with your hands.

Place a frying pan (skillet) over a medium-high heat and add enough oil to cover the base of the pan. When the oil is hot, add the cutlets and shallow-fry for 3–4 minutes on each side until golden brown. Serve hot.

snacks and small plates

# crispy rice-coated chicken strips

**Serves**
2

**Prep Time**
40 minutes

2 chicken breasts, cut into strips
4 Tbsp cornflour (cornstarch)
1 tsp salt
25g (1 cup) puffed rice
1 tsp garlic powder
1 tsp paprika
1 tsp peri peri seasoning
1 egg
1 Tbsp oil

Who doesn't love chicken strips? I know I do! But what if I told you the crispy exterior could be made with rice? You have to try these, served with a dip of your choice.

Preheat the oven to 200°C fan/220°C/425°F/Gas mark 7 and line a baking sheet with baking parchment.

Place the chicken strips in a bowl and sprinkle over the cornflour and ½ teaspoon of the salt. Toss to coat.

In a food processor, combine the puffed rice, garlic powder, paprika, peri peri seasoning and the remaining ½ teaspoon of salt. Give this a light blitz, you don't want it to be completely powdered. Transfer to a bowl.

In a separate bowl, crack the egg and whisk it.

Dip the chicken strips into the egg and then into the crispy rice mixture, making sure to really press each piece down to coat well. Lay them on the prepared baking sheet.

Drizzle the oil over the chicken strips and bake them in the oven for 15-20 minutes until the chicken is cooked through.

Serve hot with dipping sauces of your choice.

# mini veggie kimbap

**Serves**
2

**Prep Time**
40 minutes

300g (2⅓ cups) cooked short-grain rice, such as sushi rice
1 Tbsp sesame oil
½ tsp salt plus a pinch
100g (2 cups) raw spinach
1 large carrot, julienned
2 sheets of nori
2 Korean yellow pickled radish strips
1 Tbsp sesame seeds

**I must warn you... these little sushi-like rolls are highly addictive, so try at your own risk. Kimbap originates from South Korea, where this mini version is often served as a side to other main meals.**

Put the cooked rice into a bowl. Add 1 teaspoon of the sesame oil and a pinch of salt and give it a good mix.

Heat ½ teaspoon of the sesame oil in a sauté pan, add the spinach along with ¼ teaspoon of the salt and sauté over a medium heat for 2–3 minutes. Remove from the pan to a bowl and set aside.

Repeat step 2 with the carrots and another ½ teaspoon of sesame oil and ¼ teaspoon of salt.

Evenly spread the rice over the nori sheets, then add a line of carrot, spinach and a strip of Korean pickled radish to the middle of each one.

Roll the nori up tightly to enclose the filling (you might need to use a little water to seal the edges), then brush the top of the rolls with the remaining teaspoon of sesame oil and sprinkle on the sesame seeds.

Cut each roll into 4 pieces and enjoy!

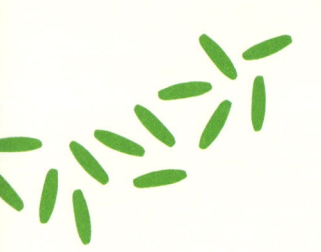

snacks and small plates

# kimchi rice balls

**Makes**
4

**Prep Time**
15 minutes

115g (¾ cup) kimchi, roughly chopped
1 tsp gochujang
260g (2 cups) cooked short-grain rice, such as sushi rice
2 tsp sesame seeds
1 tsp light soy sauce, or to taste
½ tsp caster (superfine) sugar, or to taste
¼ tsp freshly ground black pepper
¼ tsp sesame oil

**Kimchi makes everything better, in my opinion. It's a spicy fermented cabbage that is eaten at nearly every meal in South Korea. It makes even plain rice taste great! These rice balls are excellent for when you have leftover rice to use up in a hurry.**

Heat a small pan over a medium heat. Add the kimchi and gochujang and cook for 3–4 minutes, or it is slightly darkening in colour. Remove from the heat and leave to cool.

In a large bowl, combine the cooled kimchi with the rest of the ingredients. Give it a good mix, then taste. You may want to add more soy sauce or sugar to your liking.

Form into 4 balls, then enjoy.

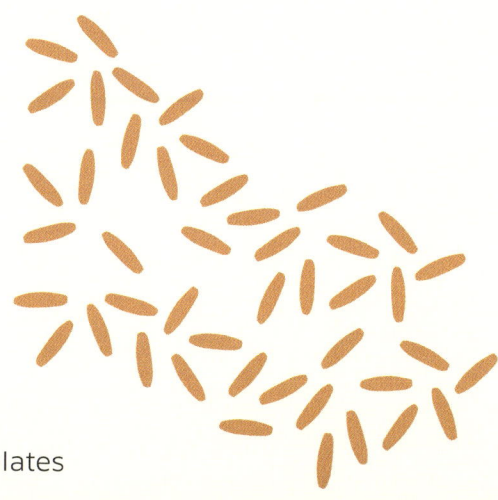

snacks and small plates

# rice flour veggie pakoras

**Serves**
4

**Prep Time**
30 minutes

1 medium potato, peeled and finely chopped into matchsticks
¼ cabbage, thinly sliced
1 small onion, finely sliced
2 green chillies, very finely chopped
10g (¼ cup) chopped fresh coriander (cilantro)
185g (1¼ cups) gram flour (besan)
4 Tbsp rice flour
1½ tsp salt, or more to taste
1 tsp chilli powder
neutral-tasting oil, such as vegetable oil, for deep-frying
ketchup or coriander chutney, to serve

**Pakoras are a teatime favourite in our house. You can make them extra crispy with just one additional ingredient – rice flour!**

Add all of the ingredients, except the oil, to a mixing bowl. Give the ingredients a really good mix with your hands. This will release some of the natural moisture from the veggies.

Now start adding water, a little at a time as needed, mixing regularly until the batter is just able to hold together without falling apart. Don't add too much water as this will stop the pakoras crisping – you will need 125–240ml (½–1 cup) of water.

Heat enough oil for deep-frying in a deep, heavy-based saucepan over a medium heat. You will know it is hot enough when a small piece of batter added to the oil sizzles immediately. In batches, fry tablespoon-sized portions of the batter for 3–4 minutes, or until golden and crispy.

Remove to drain on paper towels for a few minutes before serving with ketchup or coriander chutney.

# spicy tuna onigiri

**Makes**
4

**Prep Time**
20 minutes

160g (5¾oz) can of tuna in water, drained
2 Tbsp mayonnaise
2 Tbsp Sriracha sauce
390g (3 cups) cooked short-grain rice, such as sushi rice
2 sheets of nori, cut in half with scissors
1 Tbsp black sesame seeds

**The first time I tried these was in a convenience store in South Korea. I know that doesn't sound promising, but what if I told you I went back to get them at least eight times on my two-week trip! They make the perfect snack or lunch on the go.**

In a bowl, mix together the tuna, mayo and Sriracha.

Divide the cooked rice into 4 equal balls.

Take one of the rice balls and press it out on a piece of cling film (plastic wrap) to form a circle roughly 1cm (½in) thick.

Add a quarter of the tuna mixture to the middle of the circle of rice, then lift and twist the corners of the cling film to compress the rice into a triangle shape, making sure to enclose all of the tuna filling within the rice.

Take one of the nori sheet halves and wrap it around the base of the onigiri. Top with a sprinkle of the sesame seeds.

Repeat to make three more onigiri in the same way and enjoy!

# vietnamese rice paper 'pizza'

**Serves**
1

**Prep Time**
10 minutes

1 sheet of rice paper
1 tsp chilli oil
1 egg, lightly beaten
1 spring onion (scallion), finely chopped
1 Tbsp canned sweetcorn (corn) kernels, drained
1 Tbsp mayonnaise
1 Tbsp Sriracha sauce

On my travels around Vietnam, I came across a street vendor making these. There was a huge line of people queuing up for them, so of course I had to try one! It's a crispy, light snack that's super easy to make.

Heat a dry frying pan (skillet) over a low heat.

Add the rice paper sheet to the hot pan. Pour over the chilli oil, spreading it out evenly, then pour over the beaten egg, spreading it out to cover the rice paper.

Sprinkle the spring onions and sweetcorn on top and continue to cook until the egg is fully cooked.

To serve, drizzle over the mayo and Sriracha and tuck in.

# cheesy fried sesame balls

**Makes**
10

**Prep Time**
1 hour

130g (1 cup) glutinous rice flour, or more as needed
2 Tbsp caster (superfine) sugar
100ml (scant ½ cup) hot water, or more as needed
160g (5¾ oz) mild Cheddar cheese, cut into 10 cubes, each about 2cm (¾in) square
35g (¼ cup) white sesame seeds
neutral-tasting oil, such as vegetable oil, for deep-frying

**Known in the Philippines as *buchi*, these chewy, mochi-like balls are coated with sesame seeds and fried until slightly crispy. They are so so addictive with all that gooey melted cheese inside!**

In a bowl, mix together the glutinous rice flour and sugar, then add the hot water. Using a spatula, mix for a few minutes until the mixture begins to come together, adding more hot water or flour as needed. Once it has cooled a little, knead by hand for 4–5 minutes to form a smooth dough.

Divide the dough into 10 pieces and roll into balls.

Flatten out one of the balls and add a cube of cheese to the middle, then fold over the sides to enclose the cheese completely. Roll once again into a ball. Repeat with all of the dough and cheese cubes until you have 10 balls.

Fill a bowl with cold water and another with the sesame seeds. Dip each ball into the cold water and then immediately into the sesame seeds, making sure they are completely coated. Lightly press the sesame seeds into the balls, so they stick.

Heat enough oil for deep-frying in a deep, heavy-based saucepan over a medium heat. You will know it is hot enough when you place a wooden chopstick in the oil and it starts to sizzle slightly.

A couple at a time, fry the dough balls for 5–7 minutes until golden brown all over. Keep moving them around using a slotted spoon as you want all sides to be fully cooked. Keep an eye on them and don't let the oil get too hot or they will burn.

Now turn up the heat a little. Using your slotted spoon, hold the sesame balls down under the oil until they start to expand slightly.

Remove from the oil to drain and cool on paper towels for a few minutes, then repeat until all the sesame balls are cooked. Enjoy!

# simple weekday meals

We all know how hectic weekdays can get – juggling work, family, maybe even a workout – only to be met with the dreaded question at the end of the day, 'What's for dinner?' Well, rice has got you covered. I can guarantee that everyone has that one random bag of rice in their cupboard, so it's time to put it to use! This chapter is all about low-stress cooking that comes together quickly, but tastes amazing and isn't lacking in flavour. These recipes are going to be your midweek heroes – from one-pot wonders to cosy rice bowls, so you'll be well fed throughout the week.

# one-pan middle eastern chicken and rice

**Serves**
4

**Prep Time**
1 hour (plus 30 minutes marinating)

4 skin-on, bone-in chicken thighs
2 Tbsp olive oil
2 Tbsp Lebanese 7 spice
juice of ½ lemon
1 small onion, diced
1 aubergine (eggplant), cut into 1cm (½in) slices
350g (2 cups) raw basmati rice, washed and drained
1 chicken stock (bouillon) cube
1 tsp chilli (red pepper) flakes
sea salt and freshly ground black pepper, to taste
parsley, to garnish (optional)

Inspired by the flavours of *maqluba*, this one-pan wonder is a recipe that deserves to be on your weekly rotation. Who has the time to be washing multiple dishes after work?!

Put the chicken thighs in a bowl with 1 tablespoon of the olive oil, 1 tablespoon of the Lebanese 7 spice, the lemon juice and some salt and pepper. Mix well and leave to marinate for 30 minutes.

Heat the remaining tablespoon of oil in a large sauté pan over a medium-high heat. Add the chicken thighs and sauté for about 15 minutes, flipping them over halfway through, until almost cooked through. Remove the chicken from the pan and set aside.

To the same pan, add the onion and sauté until translucent.

Add the remaining tablespoon of Lebanese 7 spice along with the aubergine slices and sauté for 2-3 minutes.

Add the rice, crumble in the stock cube, then add the chilli flakes and sauté for another 2-3 minutes.

Add 700ml (3 cups) of water along with ½ teaspoon of salt, or more to taste, then add the chicken back to the pan and bring to the boil. Cover with a lid and cook over a low heat for 10 minutes.

Turn the heat off and leave to steam, covered, for a further 10 minutes. Garnish with parsley, if you like.

simple weekday meals

# quick and easy veg fried rice

**Serves**
2

**Prep Time**
15 minutes

2 Tbsp neutral-tasting oil, such as vegetable oil
1 small onion, finely chopped
2 garlic cloves, minced
2 small carrots, diced
2 eggs
260g (2 cups) cooked short-grain rice
4 Tbsp frozen peas
4 Tbsp light soy sauce
sea salt and freshly ground black pepper, to taste

Fried rice is a classic, in my opinion. I love all variations of it. That's one of my favourite things about it actually – it's so versatile!

Heat the oil in a wok over a medium-high heat, add the onion, garlic and carrots and stir-fry for 3–4 minutes.

Crack in the eggs and scramble.

Add the cooked rice, peas and soy sauce and season with salt and pepper. Continue to stir-fry for 4–5 minutes until all the grains of rice are evenly coated.

Serve and enjoy!

# beef pepper rice

**Serves**
2

**Prep Time**
20 minutes

4 Tbsp light soy sauce
2 Tbsp oyster sauce
2 tsp honey
2 garlic cloves, finely grated
1 tsp freshly ground black pepper
260g (2 cups) cooked short-grain rice, such as sushi rice
250g (9oz) beef steak, cut thinly against the grain
70g (½ cup) canned sweetcorn (corn) kernels, drained
1 onion, finely sliced
30g (1oz) unsalted butter
2 spring onions (scallions), sliced

**This is a Japanese recipe that makes you wonder how something can taste so good when it is so easy to make. With juicy slices of steak in a sweet and salty sauce, it's as delicious as it sounds.**

In a small bowl, mix together the soy sauce, oyster sauce, honey, garlic and black pepper. Set aside.

In a frying pan (skillet), add the cooked rice to the middle, arrange the steak slices around the rice and top with the sweetcorn and onion. Set over a medium heat, then drizzle over the sauce and add the butter. Let it cook without moving for 2–3 minutes, so the beef gets a bit crispy.

Now stir-fry until the beef is fully cooked, giving it all a good mix. Top with the sliced spring onion and serve.

# mediterranean tofu rice bowls

**Serves**
2

**Prep Time**
20 minutes

300g (10½oz) extra-firm tofu, cubed
zest and juice of 1 lemon
1 tsp thyme leaves
2 garlic cloves, minced
1 tsp olive oil
¼ tsp salt
½ tsp freshly ground black pepper
390g (3 cups) cooked white long-grain rice
2 mini cucumbers, finely sliced
½ red onion, finely sliced
10g (¼ cup) fresh parsley, chopped
30g (1oz) feta, crumbled
2–4 Tbsp Greek-style yoghurt, to serve

Here, lemony, herby, roasted tofu is piled on top of rice with crunchy red onions, fresh cucumber and herbs. Serve with a dollop of Greek-style yoghurt and you're good to go!

In a bowl, combine the tofu, lemon zest and juice, thyme, garlic, olive oil, salt and pepper. Mix until the tofu is well coated.

Heat a frying pan (skillet) over a medium-high heat, add the tofu mixture and fry for 4–5 minutes, turning until the cubes are golden brown all over.

Divide the cooked rice, cucumber, red onion and fried tofu between serving bowls and top with the parsley and crumbled feta. Serve with a dollop of yoghurt on top.

# vegan tomato rice

**Serves**
2

**Prep Time**
30 minutes

2 medium tomatoes, roughly chopped
2 green chillies, roughly sliced
1 Tbsp vegetable oil
1 tsp mustard seeds
½ tsp fennel seeds
¼ tsp fenugreek seeds
1 Tbsp chana dal (dried split chickpeas)
5-6 curry leaves
2 Tbsp cashew nuts
1 small onion, diced
1 tsp ginger and garlic paste
½ tsp salt, or to taste
½ tsp ground turmeric
1 tsp Kashmiri chilli powder
½ tsp ground coriander
1 Tbsp sambar powder (available online or in specialist Indian grocers)
60g (½ cup) frozen peas
390g (3 cups) cooked white long-grain rice
10g (¼ cup) fresh coriander (cilantro), chopped

Tomato rice is such a spicy, flavourful dish, everyone will think you spent hours making it! You can use fresh rice for this, but I always have leftover rice in my refrigerator and it's a great way to use it up along with any tomatoes you have lying around in the crisper drawer.

Put the tomatoes and green chillies into a blender or food processor and blitz to a paste.

Heat the oil in a sauté pan over a medium heat. Add the mustard seeds and when they start to pop add the fennel and fenugreek seeds, chana dal, curry leaves and cashews. Sauté for 2-3 minutes until the cashews are golden brown.

Add the onion along with the ginger and garlic paste and sauté for 3-4 minutes before adding the tomato-chilli paste and salt. Cook this down, stirring, for 6-7 minutes until the mixture slightly thickens.

Add the dried spices and cook for another 2-3 minutes, then add the peas and cook for a further 4-5 minutes.

Add the cooked rice and thoroughly mix for 1-2 minutes, so all the grains of rice are coated in the sauce, being careful not to mush up the rice.

Sprinkle the fresh coriander on top and enjoy!

# herby pork and green bean rice bowl

**Serves**
2

**Prep Time**
30 minutes

1 Tbsp vegetable oil
½ small red onion, diced
4 garlic cloves, minced
2 red chillies, minced
300g (10½ oz) minced (ground) pork
200g (7oz) green beans, cut into 2.5cm (1in) pieces
10g (¼ cup) Thai basil leaves
1 Tbsp oyster sauce
1 tsp chicken bouillon powder
1 Tbsp dark soy sauce
1 Tbsp honey
¼ tsp white pepper
260g (2 cups) cooked white jasmine or long-grain rice

**Heavily inspired by Thai *pad krapao*, this speedy meal is ready in no time. You can make it even easier for yourself by using ready-cooked microwave rice. I get it – some days are just too busy and a packet of ready-cooked rice comes in handy!**

Heat a sauté pan over a medium-high heat. Add the oil, then the red onion, garlic and chillies and sauté for 2-3 minutes.

Add the pork and sauté for 3-4 minutes.

Add the green beans, Thai basil, oyster sauce, bouillon powder, soy sauce, honey and white pepper and sauté for a further 4-5 minutes. You want the pork to get slightly charred.

Divide the rice between two bowls and serve hot, topped with the pork.

simple weekday meals

# red rice and pomegranate salad

**Serves**
2

**Prep Time**
30 minutes

2 Tbsp olive oil
juice of 1 lemon
½ tsp caster (superfine) sugar
2 garlic cloves, minced
260g (2 cups) cooked and cooled red rice
½ medium cucumber, sliced
30g (¼ cup) roasted skin-on almonds, chopped
5 spring onions (scallions), sliced
60g (¼ cup) pomegranate seeds
60g (2¼ oz) feta cheese, crumbled
10g (¼ cup) fresh mint leaves, roughly chopped
90g (3¼oz) rocket (arugula)
sea salt and freshly ground black pepper

If you're not adding rice to your salads, you are definitely missing out. The nutty, earthy flavour of red rice complements the flavours of the crispy almonds and the fresh pomegranate seeds. It's a must try!

In a small bowl, mix together the olive oil, lemon juice, sugar and minced garlic.

In a large bowl, combine all of the remaining ingredients, except the seasoning, and give them a good mix.

Drizzle over the dressing and season with salt and pepper before serving.

# one-pan peri peri chicken and rice

**Serves**
2

**Prep Time**
40 minutes (plus 30 minutes marinating)

2 chicken breasts, cut into bite-size strips
125ml (½ cup) peri peri sauce (shop-bought)
30g (1oz) butter
1 Tbsp tomato purée (paste)
½ tsp ground turmeric
½ tsp Kashmiri chilli powder
1 tsp biryani masala
1 chicken stock (bouillon) cube
175g (1 cup) raw basmati rice, washed and drained
½ tsp salt, or to taste
fresh coriander (cilantro) sprigs, to serve

This is one of my most-cooked recipes. This flavourful, zesty dish comes together before you know it and can be made in one pan. You might even end up eating more than one serving of this – I wouldn't be surprised!

In a bowl, combine the chicken with the peri peri sauce and give it a good mix. Leave to marinate for 30 minutes.

Melt the butter in a sauté pan over a medium heat. Add the chicken and sauté for 10 minutes.

Add the tomato purée and cook for 3–4 minutes, then add the turmeric, chilli powder and biryani masala and crumble in the chicken stock cube. Cook for a further 2–3 minutes.

Add the rice along with 350ml (1½ cups) of water and salt, to taste. Bring to the boil, then cover and cook over a low heat for 8 minutes.

Turn the heat off and leave to steam, covered, for a further 10–15 minutes.

Serve garnished with fresh coriander.

# south indian yoghurt rice

**Serves**
2

**Prep Time**
20 minutes

390g (3 cups) cooked and cooled long-grain white rice (I like basmati)
215-320g (1-1½ cups) plain yoghurt
1 carrot, julienned
3 Tbsp vegetable oil
1 tsp mustard seeds
1 tsp cumin seeds
2.5cm (1in) piece of fresh root ginger, finely sliced
2 green chillies, halved
2 dried red chillies
2 sprigs of curry leaves
pinch of asafoetida
2 Tbsp cashew nuts
1 tsp split skinless urad dal (black lentils)
60g (¼ cup) pomegranate seeds
salt, to taste

Yoghurt rice is a creamy, cooling dish eaten during the hot summers in India. The pops of tart sweetness from the pomegranate seeds bring freshness to a dish that is perfect for using up leftover rice.

In a bowl, mix the rice with 215g (1 cup) of the yoghurt and salt, to taste. Feel free to add more yoghurt, if you want! Add the carrot and mix well.

Heat the oil in a small saucepan over a medium heat. Add the mustard seeds and when they pop add the cumin, ginger, green chillies, dried red chillies, curry leaves, asafoetida, cashews and urad dal. Sauté for 2-3 minutes, or until the cashews are slightly golden.

Pour the mixture over the yoghurt rice and mix it in.

Serve with the pomegranate seeds sprinkled on top.

# spam, eggs and rice

**Serves**
2

**Prep Time**
10 minutes

5g (¼oz) butter
340g (11¾oz) can of Spam, cubed
2 eggs
1 Tbsp light soy sauce
1 tsp caster (superfine) sugar
260g (2 cups) cooked sushi rice (or any white rice of your liking), to serve
2 spring onions, finely sliced, to garnish (optional)
crispy chilli oil, to garnish (optional)

**I always have a can of Spam in my cupboard, along with some leftover rice in the refrigerator. They really do go hand-in-hand. Eggs? Oh, well, they just go with everything... need I say more?**

Melt the butter in a frying pan (skillet) over a medium heat. Add the Spam cubes and fry for 4–5 minutes until crisp.

Crack in the eggs and scramble. Season with soy sauce and sugar.

Serve with a steaming bowl of rice and top with spring onions and crispy chilli oil, if you like.

# prawn and mussel paella

**Serves**
4

**Prep Time**
45 minutes

1.4 litres (6 cups) hot water
1 chicken stock (bouillon) cube
¼ tsp saffron strands
3 Tbsp olive oil
1 small onion, diced
1 red (bell) pepper, diced
6 garlic cloves, minced
1 tsp smoked paprika
430g (2¼ cups) raw bomba (or arborio) rice
350g (12oz) raw peeled prawns (shrimp), tail on
300g (10½oz) fresh, shell-on mussels, cleaned
30g (¼ cup) frozen peas
sea salt and freshly ground black pepper, to taste

**To garnish**
3 Tbsp chopped fresh parsley
1 lemon, cut into wedges

Paella is a dish that originated in Valencia, Spain. It uses the locally-grown bomba, a short-grain variety of rice and there are many regional variations of the dish. This version with prawns and mussels is sure to impress.

In a large saucepan, combine the hot water, stock cube, saffron and ½ teaspoon of salt. Mix well and bring to a simmer. Bubble for 4-5 minutes, then remove from the heat and set aside.

Heat the oil in a large, deep pan over a medium heat. Add the onion and pepper and sauté for 3-4 minutes, then add the garlic and paprika and sauté for another minute.

Add the rice, hot chicken broth and a sprinkle of salt and pepper. Bring to the boil, then cover and cook over a low heat for 15-20 minutes.

After this time, remove the lid from the pan, place the prawns and mussels on top of the rice, cover again and cook for 10 minutes. The prawns should have turned pink and the mussel shells should have opened up. At this stage, add the peas and cover and cook for another 3 minutes.

Top with the parsley and garnish with lemon wedges.

# carrot and raisin pulao

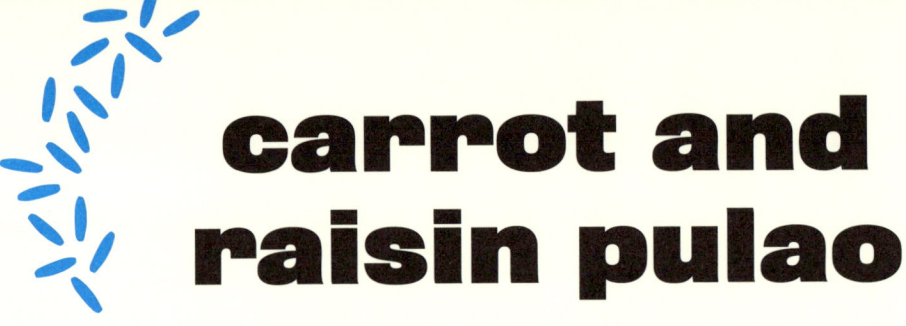

**Serves**
2

**Prep Time**
40 minutes

175g (1 cup) raw basmati rice
2 Tbsp ghee or 30g (1oz) butter
35g (¼ cup) raisins
2-3 Tbsp cashews
1 onion, finely sliced
2 carrots, sliced into matchsticks
1 tsp garam masala
½ tsp salt
350ml (1½ cups) hot water

Have you ever had rice with raisins and carrots? If your answer is no, hurry up and try this! The sweet aromas of the carrots and jammy raisins are such a great addition to this dish.

Place the rice in a bowl, cover with water and leave to soak for 10 minutes, then drain.

Meanwhile, heat the ghee or butter in a saucepan over a medium heat. Add the raisins and cashews and sauté for 3-4 minutes or until the raisins begin to puff up. Remove with a slotted spoon and set aside.

Add the onion to the same pan and sauté for 3-4 minutes until translucent.

Add the carrots and sauté for 3-4 minutes before adding the garam masala and salt.

Add the rice and sauté for 2-3 minutes, then add the raisins and cashews back to the pan.

Add the hot water and bring to the boil, then cover with a lid and cook for 10 minutes over a low heat.

Turn the heat off and leave to steam, covered, for a further 10 minutes before serving.

# harissa-roasted cauliflower and rice salad

**Serves**
2

**Prep Time**
45 minutes

1 small cauliflower, chopped into florets, leaves reserved
2 Tbsp harissa paste
2 Tbsp olive oil
55g (¼ cup) tahini
juice of ½ lemon
2 garlic cloves, finely grated
3 Tbsp hot water
260g (2 cups) cooked long-grain rice
½ cucumber, finely sliced
½ onion, finely sliced
10g (¼ cup) fresh parsley, chopped
60g (¼ cup) pomegranate seeds
sea salt and freshly ground black pepper, to taste

Harissa is a chilli paste from North Africa, which is slightly sweet and smoky thanks to ingredients such as chillies, garlic and spices. It's not super-spicy, it just adds a subtle kick to this salad.

Preheat the oven to 180°C fan/200°C/400°F/Gas mark 6.

Place the cauliflower florets and leaves in a bowl, add the harissa paste and give it a good mix.

Line a baking tray with baking parchment and spread just the cauliflower florets out on it. Drizzle with the olive oil. Roast in the oven for 30 minutes, or until the cauliflower is fully cooked. In the last 10 minutes of cooking, add the cauliflower leaves to the tray.

In a small bowl, mix together the tahini, lemon juice, grated garlic and hot water. Season with salt and pepper.

Now to assemble! You can serve in individual bowls or on a platter. Divide the rice between bowls and top with the roasted cauliflower, sliced cucumber, onion, parsley and pomegranate seeds. Drizzle with the tahini sauce and serve hot.

# thai-style basil fried rice

**Serves**
2

**Prep Time**
15 minutes

2 Tbsp vegetable oil
250g (9oz) raw peeled prawns (shrimp)
1 small onion, finely diced
4 garlic cloves, minced
2 green chillies, minced
390g (3 cups) cooked jasmine rice
handful of Thai basil leaves
2 Tbsp oyster sauce
1 Tbsp light soy sauce
1 Tbsp dark soy sauce
1 tsp caster (superfine) sugar
3 spring onions (scallions), sliced

**I do love fried rice! Here's another variation inspired by Thai flavours.**

Heat the oil in a sauté pan over a medium-high heat. Add the prawns and sauté for 1 minute on each side. Remove from the pan and set aside.

To the same pan, add the onion, garlic and chillies and sauté for 2-3 minutes.

Add the rice, Thai basil, oyster sauce, soy sauces and sugar. Sauté for a further 3-4 minutes, then add the prawns back to the pan.

Once all the grains of rice are coated, add the spring onions and serve.

# one-pot chilli beef rice

**Serves**
2

**Prep Time**
40 minutes

1 Tbsp vegetable oil
1 onion, diced
300g (10½oz) minced (ground) beef
4 garlic cloves, minced
2 green chillies, chopped
2 Tbsp tomato purée (paste)
1 red (bell) pepper, diced
2½ Tbsp fajita seasoning
180g (1 cup) raw white long-grain rice, washed and drained
¼ tsp salt, or more to taste
10g (¼ cup) fresh coriander (cilantro), chopped

Can you tell I love one-pot dishes? I always wondered why people make chilli and rice separately just to mix it up later. Why not just mix it right from the beginning? I know you will thank me for the lack of washing up!

Heat the oil in a saucepan over a medium-high heat. Add the onion and sauté for 3-4 minutes.

Add the beef, garlic and chillies and cook down for 3-4 minutes.

Add the tomato purée, red pepper and fajita seasoning and cook for another 3-4 minutes.

Add the rice along with 350ml (1½ cups) of water and salt to taste. Bring to the boil, then turn the heat to its lowest setting, cover the pan with a lid and cook for 10-12 minutes.

Turn the heat off and leave to steam, covered, for another 10 minutes.

Serve sprinkled with fresh coriander.

simple weekday meals

# tteokbokki

**Serves**
2

**Prep Time**
20 minutes

4 garlic cloves, grated
1 small onion, finely sliced
4-5 Tbsp gochujang
2 Tbsp gochugaru
1½ Tbsp caster (superfine) sugar
1 Tbsp ketchup
3 Tbsp light soy sauce
125ml (½ cup) hot water, or more as needed
500g (1lb 2oz) Korean rice cakes
2 spring onions (scallions), sliced
1 tsp sesame seeds

**I haven't met a single person who doesn't like this dish. The first time I tried these chewy rice cakes smothered in a sweet and spicy sauce, I couldn't understand how something could be so good and yet I'd never encountered a food with this texture before! I knew I had to include this recipe in the book to show just how versatile rice is.**

In a bowl, mix together the garlic, onion, gochujang, gochugaru, sugar, ketchup, soy sauce and hot water. Set aside.

Add the Korean rice cakes to a saucepan and cover with water. Bring to the boil and cook for 3 minutes, then drain off the water.

Add the sauce mixture to the rice cakes in the pan and cook down for 5-6 minutes over a medium heat. You can add extra hot water if you want it more saucy.

Serve topped with spring onions and sesame seeds.

# puttu

**Serves**
2

**Prep Time**
30 minutes

130g (1 cup) puttu rice flour (available online or in Indian grocery stores)
¼ tsp salt
40g (generous ½ cup) grated (shredded) fresh coconut
2 tsp cumin seeds

**To serve**
2 bananas, sliced
honey, for drizzling

So, I know what you're thinking... Rene, why would you suggest making this sweet-looking dish for lunch or dinner, when it's typically eaten for breakfast in south India? Well, because it's one of my guilty pleasures and if you get it, you get it! If you have a puttu steamer, that's great! But if you don't, don't worry – you can make this in little ramekins and cook in a steamer.

Add the puttu rice flour to a bowl along with the salt and 80ml (⅓ cup) water and give it a mix. The mixture will look slightly crumbly, but when you gently press it together in the palm of your hands, it should hold its shape but crumble the moment you press it firmly. You may need to add a little more water, as needed. Break it all up into fine lumps.

Prepare a steamer pan for steaming.

Divide the coconut and cumin seeds between 2 heatproof ramekins, then top with the puttu mixture. Place in the steamer and steam for 8-10 minutes.

Let them cool for 2-3 minutes before removing from the steamer.

Serve the puttu with sliced banana on the side and honey drizzled on top.

# easy roast chicken pho

**Serves**
4

**Prep Time**
1 hour

1 roast chicken, meat separated from the bones (keep the bones)
4-5 slices of fresh root ginger
1 white onion, halved
1 star anise
1 tsp coriander seeds
1 tsp black peppercorns
1 large cinnamon stick
1 chicken stock (bouillon) cube
1 Tbsp fish sauce, or to taste
salt, to taste
300g (10½oz) rice noodles
½ red onion, finely sliced
5-6 spring onions (scallions), sliced
10g (¼ cup) fresh coriander (cilantro), chopped
Sriracha and hoisin sauces, to serve (optional)

Pho is a Vietnamese noodle soup that is usually cooked down for hours and hours. I don't have hours and hours to spare, so here's a little hack on how to make it using a ready-roasted chicken!

Fill a large saucepan with 1.65 litres (7 cups) water and add the chicken bones, ginger slices, onion halves, star anise, coriander seeds, peppercorns, cinnamon stick and stock cube. Bring to the boil, then reduce the heat to medium and let it simmer for 30 minutes before straining out the solids, reserving the broth.

Season the broth with fish sauce and salt, to taste.

Bring a separate pan of water to the boil, add the rice noodles and cook for 3 minutes, then drain.

Divide the noodles between serving bowls and top with plenty of the broth, some roast chicken, red onion, spring onions and fresh coriander. Serve with Sriracha and hoisin sauce on the side, if you like.

If you have any leftovers, just store everything separately in the refrigerator and reheat when needed.

# ten-minute garlic rice noodles

**Serves**
1

**Prep Time**
10 minutes

250g (9oz) rice noodles
2 spring onions (scallions), sliced
2 garlic cloves, finely grated
½ tsp finely grated fresh root ginger
1 Tbsp chilli (red pepper) flakes (add less if you don't want it too spicy)
½ tsp caster (superfine) sugar
½ tsp paprika
1 Tbsp sesame seeds
4 Tbsp vegetable oil
1 Tbsp light soy sauce
1 tsp sesame oil
1 tsp Chinese black vinegar

**This recipe is an absolute gem. It comes together so easily and packs a fresh punch. Once you try it, you'll be making it every week. You can even change it up by using different shapes of rice noodles to find out your favourite type.**

Bring a saucepan of water to the boil and cook the rice noodles according to the packet instructions. Drain and set aside.

In a heatproof bowl, combine the spring onions, garlic, ginger, chilli flakes, sugar, paprika and sesame seeds.

Heat the vegetable oil in a small saucepan, then pour the hot oil over the ingredients in the bowl. Give it a quick mix, then add the soy sauce, sesame oil and Chinese black vinegar.

Pour over the rice noodles, mix and enjoy.

# fresh rice paper summer rolls

**Serves**
2

**Prep Time**
20 minutes

6 sheets of rice paper
1 large carrot, julienned
6 lettuce leaves
¼ red cabbage, finely sliced
½ cucumber, finely sliced
¼ onion, finely sliced
½ red (bell) pepper, finely sliced
handful of fresh mint leaves

**For the dipping sauce**
¼ cup smooth peanut butter
1 Tbsp rice vinegar
1 Tbsp maple syrup
1 tsp sesame oil
1 Tbsp light soy sauce
1 garlic clove, finely grated
1 tsp dried chilli (red pepper) flakes

Fresh, crunchy summer rolls are the perfect dish when you want something light and packed with veggies. You'll definitely be getting a good hit of fibre with these. Oh, and don't forget the peanut dipping sauce, it's a must!

Take a sheet of rice paper and dip it in water for roughly 15 seconds until softened. Place it on a plate.

Layer some of the carrot strips, lettuce, cabbage, cucumber, pepper, onion and a few fresh mint leaves in the middle of the rice paper, then roll it up tightly to enclose the filling.

Repeat until you have used up all the rice paper and fillings.

In a bowl, mix together all the ingredients for the dipping sauce along with 2 tablespoons of water. Serve alongside the fresh rolls.

# rice flour rotis

**Serves**
2 (makes 6)

**Prep Time**
45 minutes

130g (1 cup) rice flour
½ tsp salt
vegetable oil, for greasing

**This is a gluten-free recipe that never fails to amaze me. The fact that these lovely soft rotis are made from rice is just incredible!**

In a saucepan, bring 240ml (1 cup) water to the boil, then add the rice flour and give it a good mix. Turn off the heat, cover the pan and leave the dough to steam for 10 minutes.

Lightly oil your hands and knead the dough until it forms a large ball. This will take about 4–5 minutes.

Divide the dough into 6 portions. Place each portion between two sheets of baking parchment and use a rolling pin to roll them thinly, around 2mm (⅟₁₆in).

Heat a non-stick frying pan (skillet) over a medium-high heat. Cook each roti for a couple of minutes on each side, until browned in places; they may begin to puff up slightly.

Serve with any curry or stew of your choice. These don't store well, so eat immediately.

# weekend cooking

It's the weekend and you have a bit more time to chill and perhaps show off a little. I promise you that rice is going to be doing the same thing in this chapter, which is all about showcasing this brilliant grain to its full potential. It features dishes with layers of flavour, which you have to cook low and slow, that will be sure to impress. From richly spiced biryani to cheesy, decadent risotto, these recipes are a labour of love and are meant for days when you have got a bit of extra time to spare. So, if you want to be the host who's doing the most, are trying to impress a first date with your incredible cooking, or even preparing a special dish for your mum's birthday, this chapter has got you covered.

# the ultimate chicken biryani

**Serves**
5–6

**Prep Time**
2 hours 30 minutes

**For the marinated chicken**
1.2kg (2lb 10oz) skinless, bone-in chicken thighs
110g (½ cup) plain yoghurt
2 Tbsp ginger and garlic paste
2 tsp Kashmiri chilli powder
1½ tsp ground turmeric
1 tsp garam masala
1 tsp salt

**For the rice**
700g (4 cups) raw basmati rice, washed and drained
2 Tbsp ghee
1 cinnamon stick
5–6 cardamom pods
5 cloves
2 bay leaves
1.4 litres (6 cups) hot water
1½ tsp salt

If there's one meal I could eat every day, it would be biryani. I'm its biggest fan and I like to think I've mastered how to make the perfect biryani. It's a dish that can be complicated to tackle, but I've tried to break it down as much as possible so it doesn't feel as intimidating. This is best served with a yoghurt raita.

Cut each chicken thigh in half, so one piece has the bone in and one piece is boneless. Place in a large mixing bowl and add all of the marinade ingredients. Mix well, then set aside to marinate while you prepare the rice.

Put the rice in a bowl and cover with cold water. Leave to soak for 15 minutes, then drain.

Place a large, heavy-based pan over a medium heat and add the ghee along with the whole spices. Sauté for 2–3 minutes.

Add the drained rice and sauté for 3–4 minutes, then add the hot water and salt and bring to the boil. Cover, reduce the heat to low and cook for 8 minutes.

Turn the heat off and leave the rice to steam, covered, for a further 7 minutes. Use a rubber spatula to fluff up the rice and set it aside.

Now for the masala. Heat the ghee and oil in a large heavy-based casserole dish over a medium heat, add a quarter of the sliced onions and sauté until golden brown. Remove with a slotted spoon and set aside on paper towels to drain.

Add the raisins to the pan and sauté for 2–3 minutes until they puff up. Set aside with the fried onions.

Sauté the cashews the same way and set aside.

weekend cooking

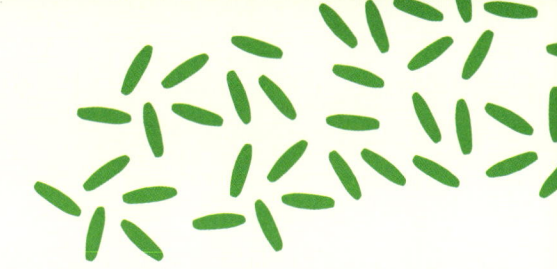

**For the masala**
2 Tbsp ghee
2 Tbsp vegetable oil
4 onions, finely sliced
35g (¼ cup) raisins
30g (¼ cup) cashews
1 cinnamon stick
4-5 cardamom pods
1 Tbsp ginger and garlic paste
4 green finger chillies, finely sliced
3 tomatoes, chopped
3 Tbsp biryani masala
20g (½ cup) fresh coriander (cilantro), chopped
10g (¼ cup) fresh mint, chopped
salt, to taste

Add the rest of the onions along with the cinnamon stick, cardamom pods, ginger and garlic paste and green chillies. Sauté for 6-7 minutes, or until the onions are soft.

Add the chopped tomatoes and sauté for 4-5 minutes.

Add the biryani masala and cook for 1 minute before adding the marinated chicken along with half the fresh coriander and mint. Mix well, cover and cook for 20 minutes, or until the chicken is fully cooked. Once done, add salt to taste and a bit of water if you think the mixture is too dry – it should look like a thick gravy.

To assemble the biryani, choose another heavy-based pan with a tight-fitting lid. Add half the chicken masala mix to the pan, then layer on half the rice. Scatter on half the remaining fresh coriander and mint, then add half the fried onions and raisins. Repeat.

Cover the biryani with a lid and let it cook over a very low heat for a final 15 minutes. Remove from the heat and gently mix the layers before serving. Enjoy!

# lamb kabuli pulao

**Serves**
4-5

**Prep Time**
1 hour 45 minutes

80ml (⅓ cup) ghee
2 carrots, sliced into matchsticks
140g (1 cup) raisins
30g (¼ cup) cashew nuts
1 onion, finely sliced
750g (1lb 10oz) boneless lamb, cubed (I usually use shoulder or neck)
½ tsp garam masala
¼ tsp ground cinnamon
¼ tsp ground cardamom
2 tsp freshly ground black pepper
2 tsp salt, or to taste
350g (2 cups) raw basmati rice, washed and drained

Many consider this the national dish of Afghanistan. It's a hearty meal made with lamb, caramelized carrots and raisins. There are not too many spices in this pulao, so the flavours of the lamb really shine through.

Melt the ghee in a saucepan over a medium heat, add the carrots and sauté for 3-4 minutes. Remove from the pan with a slotted spoon and set aside.

In the same pan, sauté the raisins for 3-4 minutes, or until they puff up, and set aside with the carrots.

Sauté the cashew nuts in the same way for 1-2 minutes and set aside.

Add the onion to the pan and sauté until golden, then add the lamb, garam masala, ground cinnamon, ground cardamom, black pepper and salt. Sauté for 4-5 minutes.

Add 455ml (2 cups) of water, cover the pan and simmer for 45 minutes, or until the lamb is tender.

Add the rice, stir and cook, covered, for 10-12 minutes.

Turn the heat off and leave the rice to steam, covered, for a further 10-12 minutes.

Serve topped with the caramelized carrots, raisins and cashews.

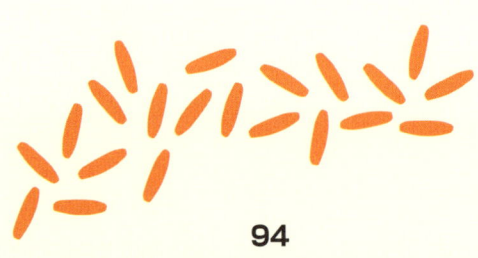

weekend cooking

# greek-style chicken, rice and lemon soup

**Serves**
2-3

**Prep Time**
1 hour

2 Tbsp olive oil
2 chicken breasts
1 onion, diced
6 garlic cloves, minced
2 carrots, diced
2 celery sticks, diced
2 bay leaves
1 tsp dried chilli (red pepper) flakes
2 tsp Italian seasoning (shop-bought)
1 chicken stock (bouillon) cube
90g (½ cup) raw white long-grain rice, washed and drained
juice of 2 lemons
2 eggs
10g (¼ cup) chopped fresh parsley
10g (¼ cup) chopped fresh dill
sea salt and freshly ground black pepper, to taste
grated Parmesan, to serve

**Sometimes all you need is a comforting soup. This Greek-inspired soup with lots of lemon and fresh herbs might be exactly what you're looking for. It's hearty and packed with flavour.**

Heat the olive oil in a saucepan over a medium heat. Add the chicken breasts and fry for 6-7 minutes on each side until cooked though. Remove the chicken, shred the meat and set aside.

To the same pan, add the onion, garlic, carrots and celery. Sauté for 4-5 minutes, or until softened.

Add the bay leaves, chilli flakes, Italian seasoning and 1.65 litres (7 cups) of water. Crumble in the stock cube. Bring to the boil, then add the chicken meat back in and simmer for 20 minutes.

Add the rice and the lemon juice, give it a stir and simmer for 10-15 minutes.

Crack the eggs into a heatproof bowl. Remove 240ml (1 cup) of the soup broth and whisk it into the eggs, then pour the mixture into the soup while stirring.

Once the rice is fully cooked, add the parsley and dill and season with salt and pepper to taste.

Serve with a sprinkle of fresh Parmesan.

# veggie bibimbap

**Serves**
4

**Prep Time**
45 minutes

8 tsp vegetable oil
2 large carrots, julienned
8 tsp minced garlic
4 tsp sesame oil
2 tsp salt, or to taste
200g (3 cups) mushrooms, sliced
2 courgettes (zucchini), finely sliced
50g (1 cup) raw spinach
180g (3 cups) beansprouts
520g (4 cups) cooked rice (sushi rice is my fave for this!)
4 Tbsp gochujang, or to taste
8 tsp toasted sesame seeds
4 large eggs, fried until crispy (optional)

**This is a Korean mixed rice and vegetable dish that's great for using up leftover rice and most of the veggies you might have in your refrigerator!**

Heat 2 teaspoons of the vegetable oil in a pan over a medium heat, add the carrots along with 2 teaspoons of the minced garlic and sauté for 2-3 minutes. You are not looking to fully cook the carrots at this stage. Stir through 1 teaspoon of the sesame oil and a pinch or two of salt, then tip out into a bowl and set aside.

Repeat step 1 with the mushrooms.

Repeat step 1 with the courgettes.

Repeat step 1 with the spinach.

Bring a saucepan of water to the boil, add the beansprouts and blanch for 1-2 minutes, then drain. Now repeat step 1 with the blanched beansprouts.

To assemble, divide the cooked rice and vegetables between bowls, then top each serving with 1 tablespoon of gochujang and 2 teaspoons of sesame seeds. You can add more or less gochujang according to taste. If you like, top each serving with a crispy fried egg. This can be served hot or cold; if serving hot, ensure the rice is piping hot. Mix everything together before eating.

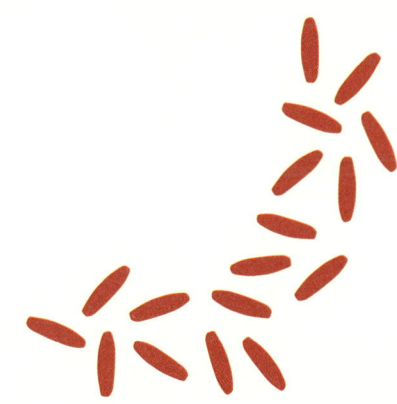

# loco moco

**Serves**
3-4

**Prep Time**
1 hour

This is a Hawaiian comfort food that's often eaten for breakfast, or just whenever you're craving it! Think juicy beef patties smothered with a mushroom and onion gravy, all on top of hot rice with a runny fried egg. Delicious!

180g (1 cup) raw jasmine rice, washed and drained
350ml (1½ cups) hot water
vegetable oil, for frying
3-4 eggs

**For the patties**
450g (1lb) minced (ground) beef
1 egg
½ onion, finely diced
1 Tbsp Worcestershire sauce
1 Tbsp light soy sauce
1½ tsp salt

**For the sauce**
30g (1oz) unsalted butter
½ onion, finely sliced
200g (7oz) mushrooms, sliced
3 Tbsp plain (all-purpose) flour
1 Tbsp light soy sauce
1½ tsp Worcestershire sauce
1 beef stock (bouillon) cube

Put the rice in a bowl and cover with cold water. Leave to soak for 15 minutes, then drain.

Add the drained rice to a saucepan along with the measured hot water and bring to the boil, then cover and cook over a low heat for 10 minutes. Turn the heat off and leave the rice to steam, covered, for a further 10 minutes.

To make the patties, place all the ingredients in a bowl and mix well. Form into 3 large or 4 smaller patties.

Heat about 2 tablespoons of vegetable oil in a frying pan (skillet) over a medium-high heat and fry the patties for about 3 minutes on each side, or until fully cooked. Remove from the pan and set aside.

Make the sauce in the same pan. Melt the butter, then add the onion and mushrooms and sauté until softened.

Add the flour and mix thoroughly, letting it cook for a minute, then add 570ml (scant 2½ cups) of water, the soy sauce and Worcestershire sauce and crumble in the stock cube. Bring to the boil, then simmer until thickened.

In a separate frying pan, heat a teaspoon of vegetable oil over a high heat and fry the eggs sunny-side up.

To serve, divide the rice between bowls and top each with a beef patty, then the mushroom sauce. Place a fried egg on top and enjoy.

# nasi goreng

**Serves**
4

**Prep Time**
20 minutes

8 garlic cloves
2 red chillies
6 shallots
2 tsp fermented shrimp paste
5 Tbsp vegetable oil
2 large skinless, boneless chicken breasts, diced
650g (5 cups) cooked jasmine rice
4 Tbsp kecap manis
2 Tbsp dark soy sauce
4 spring onions (scallions), sliced
4 eggs, fried sunny-side up (optional)

**This is an Indonesian fried rice that packs a punch. It uses shrimp paste, which is very common in Indonesian cooking. It has a strong aroma, so a little goes a long way!**

Using a pestle and mortar, pound the garlic cloves, chilli, shallots and fermented shrimp paste until a paste forms (you can also do this in a blender).

Heat the oil in a wok over a medium-high heat. Add the paste and stir-fry for 4–5 minutes, or until the oil separates and it's really fragrant.

Add the chicken and stir-fry for 4–5 minutes, or until the chicken is fully cooked.

Add the cooked rice, kecap manis and soy sauce and stir-fry for about 3–4 minutes until all the grains of rice are coated.

Serve each portion topped with spring onions and a fried egg, if liked.

# prawn risotto

**Serves**
4

**Prep Time**
50 minutes

1.5 litres (6½ cups) hot water
2 vegetable stock (bouillon) cubes
500g (1lb 2oz) raw peeled prawns (shrimp)
200g (7oz) unsalted butter
2 small white onions, diced
5 garlic cloves, minced
380g (2 cups) raw arborio rice
300ml (1¼ cups) white wine
30g (½ cup) grated Parmesan
juice of 1½ lemons
20g (½ cup) chopped fresh parsley
sea salt and freshly ground black pepper, to taste

This is a creamy prawn risotto that reminds me of a trip I made to the Amalfi coast every time I make it. I hope this brings a little bit of Italy to your home too.

In a large saucepan, mix the hot water with the stock cubes and keep warm.

Season the prawns with salt and pepper.

Melt the butter in a sauté pan over a medium heat. Add the prawns and fry for a minute on each side, then remove from the pan and set aside.

To the same pan, add the onions and garlic and sauté for 3-4 minutes until softened.

Add the rice to the pan and sauté for 2-3 minutes, then add the wine along with a ladleful of the stock and mix thoroughly until all the liquid has been absorbed. Keep adding more stock, a ladleful at a time, and stirring until the rice is cooked. This will take 30-35 minutes.

Add the prawns back to the pan along with the Parmesan, lemon juice and fresh parsley.

Mix thoroughly, then check the seasoning, adding more salt or pepper, if needed, before serving.

# vegan burrito bowl

**Serves**
4

**Prep Time**
1 hour

1 x quantity of Coriander and Lime Rice (see page 140)
2 tsp vegetable oil
1 large onion, finely sliced, plus ½ onion, diced
2 red (bell) peppers, finely sliced
400g (14oz) can of black beans in water, drained
200g (7oz) can of sweetcorn (corn), drained
½ tsp ground cumin
1 tomato, diced (or a handful of cherry tomatoes, cut into quarters)
½ iceberg lettuce, shredded
2 avocados, flesh mashed
10g (¼ cup) fresh coriander (cilantro), chopped
salt, to taste
lime wedges, to serve

**This is a veggie-packed fiesta in a bowl and a perfect way to use one of my rice side recipes!**

Make the Coriander and Lime Rice according to the recipe on page 140.

Heat 1 teaspoon of the oil in a sauté pan over a medium heat, add the sliced onion and peppers and sauté for 4-5 minutes or until slightly softened. Add a pinch of salt, then remove from the pan and set aside.

Add the remaining teaspoon of vegetable oil to the same pan, then add the diced onion and sauté for 3-4 minutes.

Add the black beans, sweetcorn, cumin, a pinch of salt and a splash of water and sauté for 4-5 minutes. Remove from the heat.

To assemble the burrito bowls, divide the rice between serving bowls, then top with the black beans and corn, then the sautéed onions and peppers. Add some diced tomato, shredded lettuce and mashed avocado, then top with some fresh coriander and serve with lime wedges.

# herby chicken bone broth with rice and crispy onions

**Serves**
4

**Prep Time**
40 minutes

2 Tbsp olive oil
4 skinless, boneless chicken breasts
5 garlic cloves, minced
5cm (2in) piece of fresh root ginger, thinly sliced
1 small onion, finely sliced
2 red chillies, finely sliced
4 carrots, thickly sliced
2 chicken stock (bouillon) cubes, crumbled
2 Tbsp miso paste
sea salt and white pepper, to taste
520g (4 cups) cooked short-grain rice

**To garnish**
20g (½ cup) crispy fried onions (shop-bought)
20g (½ cup) fresh coriander, (cilantro) chopped

This is one of those dishes that I feel heals you right down to your core. Broth and rice is one of my favourite combinations and I think you will LOVE it too!

Heat the oil in a saucepan over a medium heat. Add the chicken breasts and sear on both sides, then add the garlic, ginger, onion, chillies, carrots, stock cubes and miso. Cover with water and simmer for 30 minutes, or until the chicken is fully cooked.

Remove the chicken and shred the meat.

Taste the broth and add salt and white pepper, as needed.

Add a serving of rice to each bowl, then divide the meat between the bowls and ladle over the broth. Top with crispy onions and some fresh coriander and enjoy.

# butter chicken biryani

**Serves**
4

**Prep Time**
1 hour 30 minutes

800g (1lb 12oz) skinless, boneless chicken thighs, cut into bite-sized pieces
3½ tsp Kashmiri chilli powder
½ tsp salt, or more to taste
2 tsp ginger and garlic paste
1½ Tbsp vegetable oil, for cooking
3 onions, chopped
2 green chillies, chopped
2 tomatoes, chopped
10-12 cashew nuts
1½ tsp garam masala
½ tsp cumin seeds
1 tsp ground coriander
45g (1½oz) unsalted butter
1 tsp kasoori methi (dried fenugreek leaves)
125ml (½ cup) double (heavy) cream
1 tsp caster (superfine) sugar

This is a fusion of my two favourite dishes! This one comes together in less time than my ultimate biriyani chicken recipe (see page 90).

Put the chicken in a bowl along with 1 teaspoon of the Kashmiri chilli powder, ½ teaspoon of salt and 1 teaspoon of the ginger and garlic paste. Give this a good mix and leave to marinate while you make the rice.

Put all of the rice ingredients in a heavy-based pan along with 700ml (3 cups) of water and bring to the boil, then cover and cook over a low heat for 8 minutes.

Turn the heat off and leave the rice to steam, covered, for a further 8 minutes, then use a spatula to give the rice a gentle mix. Set aside.

Heat the vegetable oil in a sauté pan over a medium heat, then add the marinated chicken and sauté until almost cooked through. Remove from the pan with a slotted spoon and set aside.

To the same pan, add the onions, green chillies, the remaining teaspoon of ginger and garlic paste, the chopped tomatoes and the cashews. Sauté for about 4-5 minutes over a medium heat.

Add 60ml (¼ cup) of water, give it a mix, then add the remaining 2½ teaspoons of Kashmiri chilli powder along with the garam masala, cumin seeds and ground coriander. Sauté for 3-4 minutes, or until the spices are fragrant, then turn off the heat and leave to cool.

Transfer the cooled mixture to a blender and blitz until you have a smooth sauce.

*Method and ingredients continue overleaf . . .*

weekend cooking

## butter chicken biryani continued...

**For the rice**
350g (2 cups) raw basmati rice, washed and drained
1 star anise
1 cinnamon stick
4 cardamom pods
½ tsp salt

**To assemble**
10g (¼ cup) fresh coriander (cilantro), chopped
20g (½ cup) crispy fried onions (shop-bought)
80g (⅔ cup) toasted cashews

Melt the butter in a saucepan over a medium heat and add the sauce along with the chicken, kasoori methi, cream and sugar. Give everything a good mix, then cover and cook for 4–5 minutes, stirring occasionally. Taste and add more salt, if needed.

Assemble the biryani in a heavy-based pan with a tight-fitting lid. Add half the butter chicken to the bottom of the pan, then half the rice, half the fresh coriander, half the crispy fried onions and half the toasted cashews. Repeat with the remaining ingredients. Cover and let it steam over the lowest heat for 7–8 minutes.

Gently mix up the layers before serving.

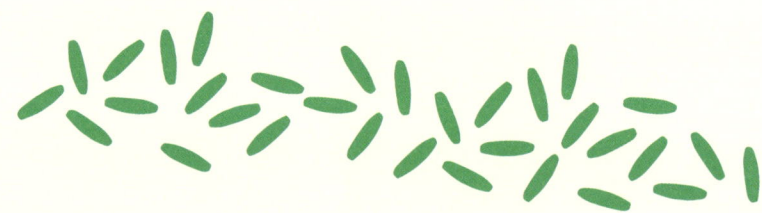

# lamb kabsa

**Serves**
4

**Prep Time**
1 hour 40 minutes

115g (1½ cups) raw basmati rice, washed and drained
1 Tbsp vegetable oil
2 onions, diced
800g (1lb 12oz) lamb, cut into cubes (any cut of lamb will do)
1 large cinnamon stick
2 bay leaves
4 cardamom pods
3 cloves
1 dried lime
½–1 tsp salt, to taste
1½ tsp kabsa spice powder (available online or in Middle Eastern grocers)
1 Tbsp tomato purée (paste)
60ml (¼ cup) passata (strained tomatoes)

**To garnish**
1 Tbsp vegetable oil
2 Tbsp raisins
3 Tbsp flaked (slivered) almonds

This is a dish that's popular across the Middle East. Each family will have their own version… and this is mine! The addition of dried lime gives the dish a citrussy tang.

Place the washed rice in a bowl, cover with cold water and leave to soak for 30 minutes, then drain.

Meanwhile, heat the oil in a sauté pan over a medium heat, add the onions and sauté for 5–10 minutes, or until they are starting to brown.

Add the lamb and sauté for 5–6 minutes until it is lightly seared on all sides.

Add the cinnamon stick, bay leaves, cardamom pods, cloves, dried lime, salt and kabsa spice powder and mix for 2–3 minutes, then add the tomato purée and passata and cook for 4–5 minutes.

Add 455ml (2 cups) of water, mix, then cover and cook over a low heat for about 45 minutes, or until the lamb is tender, stirring occasionally. If it starts to look dry, add more water as needed.

Once the lamb is tender, remove it from the pan and set it aside. Strain the broth, reserving the liquid.

Assemble the dish in a heavy-based pan that has a tight-fitting lid. Add the lamb pieces to the bottom of the pan, then add the rice. Pour over 525ml (2¼ cups) of the reserved broth from the meat. If you don't have enough broth, top it up with some water and add salt as needed. Cook over a high heat for 3–4 minutes, or until the sides are bubbling, then cover, reduce to heat to low and cook for 10 minutes.

**Method continues overleaf . . .**

## lamb kabsa continued...

Turn the heat off and leave the rice to steam, covered, for a further 10 minutes.

While it's steaming, heat the oil for the garnish in a separate pan over a medium heat, add the raisins and almonds and sauté for 2–3 minutes, or until slightly toasted.

Serve topped with the garnish.

# sri lankan coconut rice with sambal

**Serves**
4

**Prep Time**
30 minutes

2 Tbsp vegetable oil
1 tsp mustard seeds
2 whole dried red chillies
12 curry leaves
2 tsp minced fresh root ginger
2 green chillies, sliced in half
2 Tbsp cashew nuts
40g (½ cup) grated (shredded) fresh coconut
600g (5 cups) cooked white basmati rice
salt, to taste
fresh coriander (cilantro), to garnish

**Coconut sambal**
4 tsp dried chilli (red pepper) flakes
2 tsp Kashmiri red chilli powder
10 curry leaves
½ onion, finely chopped
4 garlic cloves
200g (scant 3 cups) grated (shredded) fresh coconut
juice of 1 lime
salt, to taste

Fragrant and super-easy to whip up, this dish is another great way to use up leftover rice. Grated (shredded) fresh coconut can be found in the frozen section of most large supermarkets or Asian grocers. If it's not available near you, you could use unsweetened desiccated (dried shredded) coconut as an alternative.

Heat the oil in a saucepan over a medium heat, add the mustard seeds and when they start to pop add the dried red chillies, curry leaves, fresh ginger, green chilli halves and cashews. Sauté for 1 minute.

Add the grated coconut and sauté for 3-4 minutes to soften it.

Add the cooked rice and a pinch of salt and sauté for 3-4 minutes.

Add all of the ingredients for the coconut sambal to a food processor and blitz until not completely smooth, you still want a bit of texture.

Serve the rice with the sambal, garnished with fresh coriander.

# chicken asopao

**Serves**
6

**Prep Time**
1 hour

This hearty Puerto Rican chicken and rice soup literally feels like a hug in a bowl. *Sofrito* is a flavour-boosting base of aromatics used in many Latin American cuisines. Similar to Italian *soffritto*, this version uses red and green (bell) peppers and is blended to a paste before cooking.

6 skinless, boneless chicken thighs, chopped into bite-sized pieces
1 tsp garlic powder
1 tsp paprika
1 tsp onion powder
½ tsp dried oregano
½ tsp ground cumin
½ tsp ground coriander
1 Tbsp vegetable oil
1 red (bell) pepper, diced
1 carrot, diced
2 celery sticks, diced
2 bay leaves
125ml (½ cup) passata (strained tomatoes)
1 chicken stock (bouillon) cube
270g (1½ cups) raw white long-grain rice, washed and drained
60g (½ cup) frozen peas
30g (¼ cup) pitted green olives, sliced
sea salt and freshly ground black pepper, to taste

**For the sofrito**
1 red (bell) pepper
½ green (bell) pepper
½ onion
5 garlic cloves
10g (¼ cup) fresh coriander (cilantro)

**To garnish**
10g (¼ cup) fresh coriander, (cilantro) chopped
1 lime, cut into wedges

Put the chicken in a bowl and add the garlic powder, paprika, onion powder, dried oregano, ground cumin, ground coriander and ½ teaspoon of salt. Mix well.

Add all the sofrito ingredients to a food processor and blend to a paste.

Heat the oil in a heavy-based pan over a medium heat, add the chicken and sauté for 4-5 minutes. Add the diced pepper, carrot and celery and sauté for 3-4 minutes. Add the sofrito along with the bay leaves and sauté for 3-4 minutes.

Add the passata along with 1.2 litres (5 cups) of water. Once this is simmering, add the stock cube and bring to a light boil, stirring until the stock cube is dissolved.

Mix in the rice, then taste and add salt if needed. Cover and cook for about 15 minutes, or until rice is fully cooked. You can add more water if you want the texture of the soup to be more liquid.

Add the frozen peas and sliced olives and cook for a further 1-2 minutes.

Serve with lots of fresh coriander and lime wedges for squeezing.

# braised pork belly rice

**Serves**
4

**Prep Time**
1 hour

2 Tbsp vegetable oil
6 garlic cloves, crushed
5cm (2in) piece of fresh root ginger, peeled and sliced
400g (14oz) pork belly slices, rind removed and cut into bite-sized pieces
1 tsp freshly ground black pepper
2 Tbsp dark soy sauce
2 Tbsp light soy sauce
2 Tbsp brown sugar
4 Tbsp oyster sauce
2 Tbsp Chinese cooking wine
2 tsp Chinese black vinegar
2 star anise
380g (2 cups) raw white rice (I like to use short-grain rice), washed and drained
sliced cucumber, to serve

**This Chinese-inspired dish is comforting and packed with umami deliciousness.**

Heat the oil in a heavy-based pan over a medium heat, add the garlic and ginger and sauté for 1-2 minutes until fragrant.

Add the pork belly along with the black pepper and sauté for 3-5 minutes.

Add the soy sauces, brown sugar, oyster sauce, Chinese cooking wine, Chinese black vinegar, star anise and 950ml (4 cups) of water. Cover and cook for 15 minutes.

Mix in the rice, cover, reduce the heat to low and cook for 10-12 minutes.

Turn the heat off and leave the rice to steam, covered, for a further 10 minutes.

Serve with some slices of fresh cucumber and enjoy.

# broken rice with lemongrass pork chops

**Serves**
4

**Prep Time**
1 hour 30 minutes

**For the lemongrass pork**
4 pork chops
2 shallots, minced
5 garlic cloves, minced
2 lemongrass stalks, minced very finely
4 Tbsp fish sauce
1 Tbsp brown sugar
2 Tbsp light soy sauce
2 Tbsp honey

**For the dipping sauce**
60ml (¼ cup) fish sauce
50g (¼ cup) caster (superfine) sugar
125ml (½ cup) hot water
juice of 1½ limes
2 bird's-eye chillies, chopped
4 garlic cloves, minced

**For the broken rice**
360g (2 cups) raw long-grain white rice or jasmine rice, washed and drained

**To garnish**
½ cucumber, sliced
2 tomatoes, sliced (optional)
4 eggs, boiled (optional)

**The first time I tried this was on my travels in Vietnam. I was in love! The women were grilling the pork over some hot coals and the smell was just intoxicating.**

In a mixing bowl, combine all of the ingredients for the lemongrass pork and mix to coat the chops evenly. Leave to marinate while you prepare the rest of the meal.

To make the dipping sauce, combine all of the ingredients in a small bowl and set aside.

To make the broken rice, place the rice in a bowl, cover with cold water and leave to soak for 15 minutes, then drain the water and use your hands to slightly brush the rice to break up the grains.

Add the broken rice to a pan with 455ml (2 cups) of water and bring to the boil, then cover and cook over a low heat for 10 minutes.

Turn the heat off and leave the rice to steam, covered, for a further 8 minutes.

Preheat the grill (broiler) to high and line the grill pan with foil.

Grill (broil) the pork chops for about 10 minutes on each side. Depending on the thickness of your pork chops, this might take longer, so just ensure they are fully cooked.

Serve the rice with the pork chops alongside, garnished with some sliced cucumber and tomatoes, with the dipping sauce on the side or drizzled over. Add a halved boiled egg on the side, if you like.

# crispy dosas

**These crispy rice pancakes are from southern India. You can serve them with coconut chutney, any curries of your choice or – my fave – a little bit of sugar!**

**Makes**
15–18

**Prep Time**
15 minutes (plus overnight soaking and 12 hours fermenting)

540g (3 cups) raw white long-grain rice
1 tsp fenugreek seeds
150g (1 cup) urad dal (black lentils), whole or split skinless
2 Tbsp leftover cooked white long-grain rice
2 tsp sugar
1 tsp salt
vegetable oil, for cooking

**TIP**
If the batter is struggling to ferment, mix in a pinch of dried, fast-action yeast and that should do the trick. I learned this tip from my mum.

Place the rice and fenugreek seeds in a bowl and cover with water. Place the urad dal in a separate bowl and cover with water. Leave both to soak overnight.

The next morning, drain the rice and fenugreek seeds and blitz in a blender to form a smooth batter. Transfer to a mixing bowl.

Drain the urad dal and add to the blender along with the cooked rice and sugar. Blitz to form a smooth batter, adding a splash of water if needed to help it loosen.

Add the blended urad dal along with the salt to the mixing bowl with the rice batter and mix well. It should be the consistency of cake batter – not too thick but not too thin.

Cover with cling film (plastic wrap) and leave to ferment in a warm place for 12 hours. Depending on the heat, it may ferment quicker, so check on it every few hours to see if it has risen and if you can see bubbles in the batter.

When you are ready to cook, heat a frying pan (skillet) over a medium-high heat. Sprinkle a tiny bit of oil on the pan, then add a ladleful of batter and use the back of the ladle to spread it out into a circle, starting from the middle and working outwards. Drrizzle over another teaspoon of oil and cook until it starts to crisp up, then flip and crisp up for another minute.

Repeat until you have used up all the batter.

Serve hot with your favourite coconut chutney or curries, or both!

# mushroom risotto

**Serves**
4

**Prep Time**
1 hour

1.5 litres (6¼ cups) hot water
2 vegetable stock (bouillon) cubes
4 Tbsp olive oil
30g (1oz) unsalted butter
2 small white onions, diced
8 garlic cloves, minced
380g (2 cups) raw arborio rice
800g (1lb 12oz) mushrooms, sliced
20g (½ cup) fresh parsley, chopped
30g (½ cup) grated Parmesan
sea salt and freshly ground black pepper, to taste

**This dish, to me, is pure comfort. With the umami flavours from the mushroom and the Parmesan... it just doesn't get cosier than this.**

In a large saucepan, mix the hot water with the stock cubes and keep warm.

Heat the olive oil and butter in a sauté pan over a medium heat, add the onions and garlic and sauté for 3-4 minutes until softened.

Add the rice to the pan and sauté for 2-3 minutes before adding the sliced mushrooms. Sauté for another 2-3 minutes.

Add a ladleful of stock and mix thoroughly until all the liquid has been absorbed.

Keep adding more stock, a ladleful at a time, and stirring until the rice is cooked. This will take 30-35 minutes.

Add the fresh parsley and Parmesan and season with salt and pepper to taste. Serve immediately.

# idli

**Makes**
15-20

**Prep Time**
15 minutes (plus overnight soaking and 12 hours fermenting)

1 quantity Dosa batter (page 125)
neutral-tasting oil, such as vegetable oil, for greasing and frying
handful of fresh curry leaves
coconut chutney (shop-bought), to serve

**These steamed rice cakes are actually made with the same dosa batter as on page 125. They are typically eaten with sambar, which is a veggie curry, but you can have them with any curry or sauce of your choice. You will need an idli steamer to make this recipe.**

Make the dosa batter according to the instructions on page 125, following steps 1-5.

Grease the moulds of the idli steamer with a little oil, then fill each mould with batter. Fill the steamer with about 455ml (2 cups) of water, then bring to the boil over a medium heat. Add the moulds, cover and steam the idli for 10-15 minutes. A toothpick should come out clean when inserted.

Meanwhile, make the crispy curry leaves. Heat 1cm (½in) of oil to a frying pan (skillet) over a medium-high heat. Add the curry leaves and fry until they begin to crisp up, around 3 minutes. Drain on kitchen paper.

Remove the idli from the moulds before serving with the crispy curry leaves and some coconut chutney.

# ban xeo

**Serves**
6

**Prep Time**
1 hour (plus 30 minutes resting)

neutral-tasting oil, such as vegetable oil, for frying
800g (1lb 12oz) raw, peeled prawns (shrimp)
1 onion, finely sliced
200g (7oz) beansprouts

**For the batter**
50g (½ cup) cornflour (cornstarch)
130g (1 cup) rice flour
¼ tsp ground turmeric
½ tsp salt
60ml (¼ cup) full-fat coconut milk
455ml (2 cups) cold sparkling water
5-6 spring onions (scallions), finely chopped

**For the dipping sauce**
60ml (¼ cup) fish sauce
50g (¼ cup) caster (superfine) sugar
125ml (½ cup) hot water
juice of 1½ limes
2 bird's-eye chillies, chopped
4 garlic cloves, minced

**To serve**
lettuce leaves
fresh coriander (cilantro) leaves
fresh mint leaves

These Vietnamese crispy pancakes with prawns are another dish I was wowed by on my travels! Who knew rice could be used in so many different ways?

To make the batter, whisk together all the batter ingredients in a bowl and set aside to rest for about 30 minutes.

Meanwhile, make the dipping sauce. Mix all the dipping sauce ingredients in another bowl and set aside.

Heat a 25cm (10in) non-stick frying pan (skillet) over a medium heat. Add 2-3 teaspoons of oil, then add in a few prawns and sauté for 1-2 minutes until cooked (depending on the size of the prawns). Add a few slices of onion and spread across the pan evenly.

Pour in a ladleful of batter, just enough to cover the prawns and the entire base of the pan. Cook for 3-4 minutes until the edges of the pancake are crispy and start to slightly peel away.

Add a handful of the beansprouts to one side of the pancake, cover the pan with a lid or a baking tray and steam for 2-3 minutes, or until they have slightly wilted and softened.

Fold the other side of the pancake over to cover the beansprouts and remove from the pan. Set aside and keep warm.

Repeat with the remaining batter and ingredients until you have 6 pancakes.

Serve with lettuce and fresh herbs tucked inside each pancake and dip into the dipping sauce before eating.

# perfect sides

It's not news that rice makes the perfect side – it's great for soaking up sauces and balancing out flavours, no matter what it's served alongside. But it's not just about the perfect bowl of plain rice (see my No-Fail White Rice recipe on page 134) – the possibilities really are endless! The recipes in this chapter are like those supporting roles that end up stealing the show.

We're talking fragrant Ghee Rice (page 137) that's gently spiced, zesty Coriander and Lime Rice (page 140) that's going to leave people asking for seconds, and other golden classics that are oh so needed at the dinner table. If you're looking for some backups for your main act, this chapter is for you.

# no-fail white rice

**Serves**
4

**Prep Time**
25 minutes

350g (2 cups) raw basmati rice

**This is the classic. Everyone should know how to cook no-fail white rice and this method has never failed me! It goes perfectly with so many dishes and is something you just have to master.**

Wash the rice in a fine sieve (strainer) several times until the water runs clear.

Add the drained rice to a heavy-based saucepan, then add 700ml (3 cups) of water. Bring to the boil, then cover and cook over the lowest heat for 8–10 minutes.

Turn the heat off and leave the rice to steam, covered, for a further 10 minutes.

Fluff up lightly using a rubber spatula (this helps to prevent the grains of rice from breaking) and serve.

# ghee rice

**Serves**
4

**Prep Time**
30 minutes

3 Tbsp ghee
2 cinnamon sticks
1 star anise
4 cloves
4 cardamom pods
2 bay leaves
1 onion, finely sliced
1 tsp ginger and garlic paste
350g (2 cups) raw basmati rice, washed and drained
700ml (3 cups) hot water
2 Tbsp cashew nuts
2 Tbsp raisins
salt, to taste

**This is a super-flavourful, decadent rice that goes perfectly with most Indian main dishes. The subtle flavours of the whole spices and cashews make this an addictive side!**

Heat a heavy-based saucepan over a medium heat, add the ghee, then add the whole spices along with the sliced onion and ginger and garlic paste. Sauté until the onions are golden brown.

Add the rice and sauté for 3–4 minutes, or until the grains of rice are slightly toasted.

Add the hot water and salt to taste, bring to a light boil, then cover and cook over a low heat for 8–10 minutes.

Turn the heat off and leave the rice to steam, covered, for a further 10 minutes.

Top with the cashews and raisins, then serve.

# garlic butter rice

**Serves**
4

**Prep Time**
30 minutes

60g (2¼oz) unsalted butter
8 garlic cloves, minced
360g (2 cups) raw jasmine rice, washed and drained
1 tsp salt

**This is comfort food at its finest. I know this is meant to be a side, but honestly, a bowl of this garlic-infused buttery rice is just as good as a main meal for those days when I'm too lazy to cook anything else!**

Heat the butter in a saucepan over a medium heat. Once melted, add the garlic and sauté for 2-3 minutes, or until the garlic is slightly golden and fragrant.

Add the rice and sauté for a further 4-5 minutes, or until the rice starts to get slightly toasted.

Add 700ml (3 cups) of water along with the salt and bring to the boil over a high heat, then cover and cook over the lowest heat for 10 minutes.

Turn the heat off and leave the rice to steam, covered, for a further 10 minutes.

Fluff up the rice with a fork and enjoy!

# mexican-style spicy rice

**Serves**  **Prep Time**
4  30 minutes

2 Tbsp olive oil
1 large white onion, diced
5 garlic cloves, minced
360g (2 cups) raw white long-grain rice, washed and drained
2 Tbsp tomato purée (paste)
1 tsp salt
½ tsp freshly ground black pepper
½ tsp chilli powder
½ tsp ground cumin
1 chicken stock (bouillon) cube
700ml (3 cups) hot water
40g (⅓ cup) frozen peas
juice of 1 lime
10g (¼ cup) chopped fresh coriander (cilantro)

A classic at any fiesta, this style of rice was served as a side to so many of the dishes I tried in Mexico. Tacos, mole, birria… you name it! This spicy rice just goes with it all.

Heat the oil in a large saucepan over a medium heat, add the onion and garlic and sauté for about 5 minutes until softened.

Add the rice, along with the tomato purée, salt, pepper, chilli powder and ground cumin. Sauté for 3-4 minutes, or until all of the ingredients are fragrant. Take care not to let it burn.

In a jug, dissolve the chicken stock cube in the hot water, then add this to the rice along with the frozen peas. Bring to the boil over a high heat, then cover and cook over a low heat for about 10 minutes, or until all the liquid has been absorbed.

Turn the heat off and leave the rice to steam, covered, for a further 10 minutes.

Stir in the lime juice and coriander and enjoy!

# coriander and lime rice

**Serves**  **Prep Time**
4  30 minutes

360g (2 cups) raw jasmine rice, washed and drained
2 Tbsp olive oil
1 chicken stock (bouillon) cube
700ml (3 cups) hot water
½-1 tsp salt, to taste
juice of 1 lime
10g (¼ cup) chopped fresh coriander (cilantro)

This zesty, refreshing side dish is a great addition to any dinner table.

Heat the oil in a saucepan over a medium-high heat, add the rice and sauté it until it becomes slightly translucent.

In a jug, dissolve the stock cube in the hot water, then add this to the rice. Bring to the boil, then mix well and add salt. Cover and cook over the lowest heat for 8-10 minutes.

Turn the heat off and leave the rice to steam, covered, for a further 10 minutes.

Mix in the lime juice and coriander and dig in.

# south indian lemon rice

**Serves**
4

**Prep Time**
10 minutes

2 Tbsp neutral-tasting oil, such as vegetable oil
2 tsp black mustard seeds
2 tsp split skinless urad dal (black lentils)
70g (½ cup) unsalted peanuts
4 sprigs of curry leaves
4 green chillies, sliced
5cm (2in) piece of fresh root ginger, finely grated
2 tsp ground turmeric
480g (4 cups) cooked basmati rice (or any cooked long-grain white rice)
1 tsp salt, or to taste
4–5 Tbsp lemon juice, to taste
20g (½ cup) chopped fresh coriander (cilantro)

Another classic in my household, this lemon rice is absolutely delicious both on its own and as a side. It's even better made with day-old leftover rice. I just know you're going to love this one!

Heat the oil in a heavy-based pan over a medium heat, then add the mustard seeds. Once they start to pop, add the urad dal, peanuts, curry leaves, green chillies and ginger. Sauté for 3–4 minutes, or until the peanuts are roasted.

Add the turmeric and sauté for a further 30 seconds before adding the cooked rice, salt and lemon juice according to your taste. Keep stirring for a further 2–3 minutes.

Top with chopped fresh coriander before serving.

# chilli oil egg-fried rice

**Serves**
2

**Prep Time**
10 minutes

30g (1oz) butter
2 spring onions (scallions), chopped
2 eggs
2 Tbsp crispy chilli oil, or to taste
1 Tbsp light soy sauce
½ tsp white pepper
260g (2 cups) cooked rice (ideally sushi rice, but any rice works)

**This is an amped-up version of a classic egg-fried rice with a magic ingredient – crispy chilli oil! Trust me, this stuff is delicious. Serve with any Chinese meal and you have an instant crowd pleaser. It is easily doubled to serve four, but is best cooked in batches as described, so as not to overcrowd the pan.**

Melt the butter in a frying pan (skillet) over a medium heat, then add the spring onions and sauté for 2 minutes.

Crack in the eggs and scramble. Season with the chilli oil, soy sauce and white pepper.

Add the rice and stir-fry for a further 2–3 minutes.

# black pepper rice

**Serves**
4

**Prep Time**
10 minutes

6 garlic cloves
3 Tbsp black peppercorns
2 Tbsp neutral-tasting oil, such as vegetable oil
2 tsp mustard seeds
4 sprigs of curry leaves
20 cashew nuts
480g (4 cups) cooked basmati rice
salt, to taste

**This peppery rice is something my mum used to whip up when she needed a side to a more simple main, but it's another one that I think is amazing as a main meal when you're in a rush and only have time to make one thing. The crunch of the cashews is great with the flavour of fresh pepper.**

Using a pestle and mortar, pound the garlic and peppercorns to a rough paste.

Heat the oil in a saucepan over a medium heat. When hot, add the mustard seeds. As soon as they start to pop, add the garlic and peppercorn paste along with the curry leaves. Sauté for 3–4 minutes, or until everything is fragrant and slightly toasted.

Add the cashews along with the cooked rice and season with salt to taste. Stir-fry for 3–4 minutes.

# fragrant coconut rice

**Serves**
4

**Prep Time**
25 minutes

1 tsp coconut oil
360g (2 cups) raw jasmine rice, washed and drained
400ml (1¾ cups) coconut milk
1 tsp caster (superfine) sugar, or to taste
1 tsp salt, or to taste

The creamy flavours of coconut and fragrant jasmine rice are like a match made in heaven. The perfect pairing for Asian or Caribbean dishes.

Heat a heavy-based pan over a medium heat, then add the coconut oil along with the rice and sauté for 2-3 minutes.

Add the coconut milk along with 350ml (1½ cups) of water, the sugar and salt. Give this a mix, then taste to see if you would like more salt or sugar.

Bring to the boil, then cover and cook over a low heat for 10-11 minutes.

Turn the heat off and leave the rice to steam, covered, for a further 10 minutes.

Lightly fluff up the rice before serving.

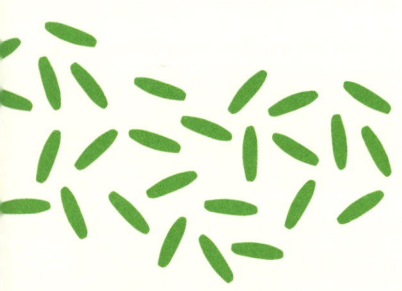

# golden turmeric rice

**Serves**
4

**Prep Time**
25 minutes

350g (2 cups) raw basmati rice, washed and drained
15g (½oz) butter
½ tsp ground turmeric
1 vegetable stock (bouillon) cube
700ml (3 cups) hot water
salt, to taste

**Another classic, just elevated! The golden grains of rice add brightness to any dish and go well with main dishes from nearly every country.**

Heat a heavy-based pan over a medium heat. Add the butter, then add the turmeric and rice. Sauté for 3-4 minutes, or until the rice is slightly toasted.

In a jug, dissolve the stock cube in the hot water, then add to the rice along with salt, to taste. Bring to the boil, then cover and cook on the lowest heat for 8-10 minutes.

Turn the heat off and leave the rice to steam, covered, for a further 10 minutes.

Give it a good mix before serving.

# easy tahdig

**Serves**
4

**Prep Time**
1 hour

2 ice cubes
a pinch of saffron strands
350g (2 cups) raw basmati rice, washed and drained
1-1½ tsp salt, to taste
4 Tbsp neutral-tasting oil, such as vegetable oil
60g (2½oz) unsalted butter, melted
pomegranate seeds, to garnish (optional)

This Iranian classic left an impression on me the moment I tried it. The crispy top with the fluffy rice underneath is a combo you don't want to miss. It's perfect served with *ghormeh sabzi* (a herby meat stew).

Place the ice cubes in a small bowl, sprinkle the saffron on top and leave to melt.

Soak the washed and drained rice in cold water for 15 minutes, then drain.

In a large saucepan, bring 950ml-1.2 litres (4-5 cups) of water to the boil (you need enough water to fully cover the rice). Add the rice and salt and cook for 7 minutes, or until the grains are tender on the outside but still firm in the middle.

Drain the rice, then cool it under running cold water to stop the cooking process.

Scoop out about ½ cup of the rice and mix it with the saffron water.

Pour the oil into a high-sided non-stick pan with a lid, then add the saffron rice and press it down to cover the base of the pan. Lightly layer the plain white rice on top. With the back of a spoon, make 4-5 holes in the rice, making sure not to reach the bottom of the pan. Drizzle over the melted butter, cover the top of the pan with a clean tea (dish) towel and place the lid on top. Cook over a low heat for 20 minutes.

Increase the heat to high and cook for a final 4-5 minutes.

Turn the heat off and leave the rice to steam, covered, for a further 5-8 minutes.

Uncover, then carefully invert the pan over a serving dish. The rice should have a crispy layer on the top. It's now ready to serve. Scatter with a few pomegranate seeds, if you like.

perfect sides

# turkish rice with vermicelli

**Serves**
4

**Prep Time**
30 minutes

3 Tbsp olive oil
25g (½ cup) vermicelli pasta, broken into small pieces
360g (2 cups) raw white long-grain rice, washed and drained
1 chicken stock (bouillon) cube
750ml (3¼ cups) hot water
½ tsp salt, or to taste

**This side is one of my favourite parts of going to a Turkish restaurant. It also is a great accompaniment to most mains, including Greek, Indian and even Middle Eastern dishes.**

Heat the oil in a heavy-based pan over a medium-high heat. Add the vermicelli and sauté for 2–3 minutes until golden brown.

Add the rice and sauté for 2–3 minutes.

In a jug, dissolve the stock cube in the hot water, then add to the rice along with salt, to taste. Bring to the boil, then cover and cook over a low heat for 10–11 minutes.

Turn the heat off and leave the rice to steam, covered, for a further 10 minutes.

Fluff up the rice gently with a fork and serve.

# spicy rice and peas

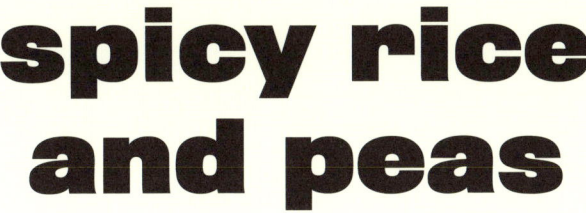

**Serves**
4

**Prep Time**
30 minutes

240ml (1 cup) coconut milk
400g (14oz) can of red kidney beans, drained
1 Tbsp all-purpose seasoning
1 tsp allspice
2 spring onions (scallions), chopped
1 Scotch bonnet chilli, left whole
1 tsp salt, or to taste
350g (2 cups) raw basmati rice, washed and drained

**Rice and peas is an iconic part of any Jamaican meal. In Jamaica 'peas' can refer to any legume – here, it's kidney beans. This is my easy version: it's just as tasty!**

Place a heavy-based pan over a medium heat and add the coconut milk along with 455ml (2 cups) of water, the kidney beans, all-purpose seasoning, allspice, spring onions, Scotch bonnet and salt, to taste. Give this all a good stir, then add the rice.

Bring to the boil, then cover and cook over a low heat for 12–14 minutes.

Once all the liquid has been absorbed, turn the heat off and leave the rice to steam, covered, for a further 10 minutes.

Fluff up with a fork and enjoy!

# sweet endings

If you thought that rice had done it all, I hope you saved space for dessert! This chapter explores the sweeter side to rice – it doesn't have to be savoury all the time. From silky rice puddings to crispy rice treats, this chapter has something for everyone with a sweet tooth – there are even ice lollies! And as I like to say: there is ALWAYS room for dessert!

# strawberry cream mochi

**Makes**
6

**Prep Time**
20 minutes (plus
45 minutes cooling)

100g (¾ cup) glutinous rice flour
25g (¼ cup) cornflour (cornstarch), plus extra for dusting
4 Tbsp caster (superfine) sugar
180ml (¾ cup) milk
20g (¾oz) unsalted butter
240ml (1 cup) double (heavy) cream
6 large strawberries, chopped into bite-size pieces

**The light and chewy texture of mochi with juicy strawberries is so delicious. This is best made in summertime with fresh berries.**

In a microwave-safe bowl, mix together the glutinous rice flour, cornflour and 2 tablespoons of the sugar until well combined. Add the milk and whisk until there are no lumps.

Cover the bowl with cling film (plastic wrap) and poke a couple of holes in it to let steam escape. Microwave on high for 3½ minutes, then carefully remove the cling film.

Add the butter to the rice mixture and mix thoroughly with a spatula or transfer to a stand mixer and mix until fully combined. It might look like as though it won't mix at first, but keep going and it will come together. Cover and place in the refrigerator to cool for about 45 minutes.

In a mixing bowl, combine the cream with the remaining 2 tablespoons of sugar. Whip until stiff peaks form. Fold in the chopped strawberries.

Dust your work surface with cornflour, turn out the mochi dough onto it and cut into 6 portions. Roll each portion out into a round, flat sheet (use a knife to cut it into a round, if necessary). Divide the whipped cream and strawberries into 6 portions and place in the middle of each circle of dough. Fold up the sides of the dough to fully enclose the filling and pinch to seal the edges.

Best served immediately or store in the refrigerator until ready to serve.

# cheat's mango sticky rice

**Serves**
2

**Prep Time**
20 minutes

400ml (14oz) can of full-fat coconut milk
50g (¼ cup) caster (superfine) sugar, or to taste
300g (10½oz) packet of microwave sticky rice
1 mango, peeled, stone removed and flesh thinly sliced
1 Tbsp toasted sesame seeds

**Mango sticky rice was my number one dessert on my travels in Thailand. This is a hack version for when you have a craving for it and want it QUICK!**

Combine the coconut milk and sugar in a saucepan and heat, stirring, over a medium heat. Make sure there are no lumps and bring to a light simmer for 5–10 minutes. You want it to thicken slightly. If you want it sweeter, feel free to add more sugar.

Meanwhile, microwave the sticky rice according to the packet instructions.

Transfer the rice to a bowl and add three-quarters of the sweet coconut milk. Let it sit for 5 minutes until the liquid has been absorbed.

Divide the rice between two serving plates and arrange a few mango slices on the side of each serving. Drizzle with the remaining sweet coconut milk, sprinkle over the toasted sesame seeds and enjoy.

# rice pudding ice lollies

**Makes**
6

**Prep Time**
30 minutes (plus overnight freeze)

190g (1 cup) raw white long-grain rice, washed and drained
1 cinnamon stick
1 Tbsp vanilla extract
570ml (scant 2½ cups) full-fat milk, or as needed
125ml (½ cup) evaporated milk
125–185ml (½–¾ cup) sweetened condensed milk

I tried these from a street vendor on my travels in Mexico. Think rice pudding, but smooth and super super cold. Delicious! You will need 6 ice-lolly (popsicle) moulds and lolly sticks to make this.

In a saucepan, combine the rice with 455ml (2 cups) of water and add the cinnamon stick. Cook over a medium heat for about 15 minutes, or until the rice is cooked and most of the water has been absorbed. Remove the cinnamon stick.

In a blender, combine the vanilla, full-fat milk and evaporated milk with three-quarters of the cooked rice and 125ml (½ cup) of the sweetened condensed milk. Blend well. Taste, and if you think it needs more sweetness at this point, add more condensed milk, or if it is looking too thick, add more milk and blend again.

Place 1 heaped teaspoon of the remaining cooked rice into each ice-lolly mould. Top up each mould with the blended mixture and add the lolly sticks. Freeze overnight until fully set.

To release the lollies from the moulds, gently run them under warm water for a few seconds.

# indian rice pudding brûlée

**Serves**
4

**Prep Time**
1 hour 25 minutes

95g (½ cup) raw white basmati rice, washed and drained
1 Tbsp ghee
500ml (generous 2 cups) full-fat milk
60ml (¼ cup) sweetened condensed milk (add more or less to your liking)
3 cardamom pods, crushed
4 Tbsp brown sugar

**My mum's Indian rice pudding is one of my favourite desserts. This recipe takes it a step further with a crunchy brûlée topping.**

Place the washed rice in a bowl and cover with water. Leave to soak for 30 minutes, then drain.

Melt the ghee in a saucepan over a medium heat. Add the drained rice and cook for 3-4 minutes until toasted.

Add the milk, sweetened condensed milk and cardamom pods. Mix, then taste. If you prefer it sweeter, add more condensed milk to your liking. Keep stirring until the rice is fully cooked and the mixture has thickened, around 20-25 minutes. Remove from the heat and leave to cool slightly.

Divide the rice pudding between four ramekins and sprinkle a tablespoon of brown sugar on top of each one. Use a kitchen blow torch to scorch the top of each pudding until the sugar melts and browns. Alternatively, place under a hot grill (broiler).

Allow the puddings to cool and the sugar to harden before serving.

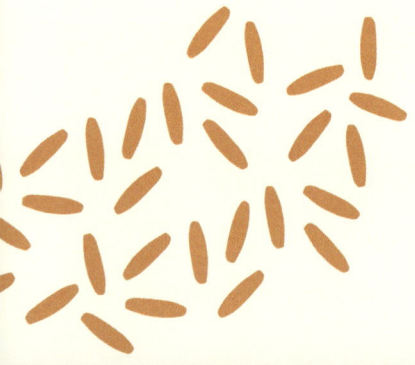

# crispy rice paper banana rolls with chocolate dip

**Makes**
4

**Prep Time**
15 minutes

1 large banana, peeled
4 sheets of rice paper
4 tsp brown sugar
15g (½oz) salted butter
chocolate spread, for dipping

I came up with this after I had a pack of rice paper to use up and I was craving a sweet treat.

Slice the banana in half widthways, then halve each piece lengthways.

Dip a sheet of rice paper in water for 15-20 seconds until softened, then lay it flat on a plate.

Sprinkle 1 teaspoon of the brown sugar in the middle of the sheet, then add 1 slice of banana. Wrap each side of the rice paper over the banana until it is fully enclosed.

Repeat steps 2 and 3 until you have 4 rolls.

Heat the butter in a non stick frying pan (skillet) over a medium heat. Fry the rolls on each side for 2-3 minutes.

Serve hot with a small bowl of chocolate spread on the side, for dipping.

# chewy mochi brownies

**Makes**
9

**Prep Time**
1 hour 20 minutes

130g (1 cup) glutinous rice flour
225g (1 cup plus 2 Tbsp) caster (superfine) sugar
50g (½ cup) cocoa powder (unsweetened)
1½ tsp baking powder
pinch of salt
85g (3oz) unsalted butter, melted
1 tsp vanilla extract
2 medium eggs
320ml (1¼ cups) milk
sea salt flakes, to finish

**Chewy, gooey and so so delicious, the texture of these are unlike any brownie you will have tried before.**

Preheat the oven to 170°C fan/190°C/375°F/Gas mark 5 and line a 20cm (8in) square baking tin with baking parchment.

In a bowl, mix together the glutinous rice flour, sugar, cocoa powder, baking powder and salt.

In a separate bowl, mix together the melted butter, vanilla, eggs and milk until well combined.

Add the wet ingredients to the dry ingredients and whisk until fully combined.

Pour the batter into the prepared tin and bake for 50 minutes- 1 hour, or until a toothpick inserted in the middle comes out with just a few moist crumbs – it shouldn't be fully wet.

Leave to cool completely before cutting into 9 squares and serving with a sprinkle of sea salt flakes on top.

# brown butter and miso crispy rice treats

**Makes**
20

**Prep Time**
20 minutes (plus 1 hour cooling)

170g (6oz) unsalted butter
600g (15 cups) mini marshmallows
1 tsp white miso
½ tsp vanilla extract
¼ tsp salt
230g (9½ cups) puffed rice cereal (such as Rice Krispies)

These are traditional puffed rice treats but with an extra nutty kick of flavour!

Line the base and sides of a deep 23 x 33cm (9 x 13in) baking tin with baking parchment.

Gently melt the butter in a very large saucepan over a medium heat for 5-6 minutes until it browns – just keep an eye on the butter, it will start to smell nutty and you will see the milk solids separate and turn golden brown.

Turn the heat down to low and add the marshmallows, miso, vanilla and salt. Stir until fully melted and combined.

Add the puffed rice cereal and mix until it is all fully coated in the buttery marshmallow mixture.

Spread the mixture over the base of the baking tin, pressing it down lightly, and leave to cool for 1 hour.

Cut into squares and serve or store in an airtight container for up to 3 days.

# chocolate and peanut butter crispy rice bites

**Makes**
6

**Prep Time**
10 minutes (plus 20 minutes chilling)

5 plain puffed rice cakes
6 pitted dates
3 Tbsp peanut butter, or as needed
100g (3½oz) plain (dark) or milk chocolate, melted
pinch of sea salt flakes

**These are great to make ahead to grab from the refrigerator whenever you need a little sweet treat.**

Add the rice cakes, pitted dates and peanut butter to a food processor and blitz until the ingredients are fully combined and have started to form a dough-like consistency. If it looks dry, add in some more peanut butter and blitz again.

Scoop the dough into 6 portions and roll into balls.

Drizzle some melted chocolate on top of each ball and add a sprinkle of sea salt.

Leave to set for 20 minutes in the refrigerator before serving.

# filipino-style sticky rice cake

**Serves**
8–10

**Prep Time**
1 hour 20 minutes

380g (2 cups) raw glutinous rice, washed and drained
700ml (3 cups) full-fat coconut milk
200g (1 cup) soft dark brown sugar
1 tsp vanilla extract
1 tsp coconut oil
1 fresh banana leaf (see Tip) or a sheet of baking paper

**TIP**
To make the banana leaf shiny and more flexible, run it over a flame on the hob or blow-torch it for a few seconds.

When I used to work as a nurse, one of my Filipino co-workers made this and let me try it. Known in the Philippines as *biko*, it's incredibly decadent and the caramel-like flavours are so so good.

Add the rice to a saucepan, then add 290ml (1¼ cups) of water and 240ml (1 cup) of the coconut milk. Give this a good mix and bring to a simmer over a medium heat.

Turn the heat to low, cover and cook for about 15 minutes, or until all the liquid has been absorbed and the rice is almost fully cooked, stirring occasionally. Remove from the heat.

In a separate large saucepan, combine the remaining coconut milk with the brown sugar and vanilla and mix well. Cook over a medium heat, stirring, for 5–10 minutes, or until the mixture is thick, golden and syrupy.

Remove 60ml (¼ cup) of the syrup and set it aside.

Add the cooked rice to the pan of syrup and gently mix continuously over a low heat for about 10 minutes, or until everything is fully combined and the rice has absorbed the extra liquid. Remove from the heat.

Preheat the oven to 180°C fan/200°C/400°F/Gas mark 6. Grease a 20cm (8in) square baking tin with the coconut oil and line with the fresh banana leaf (or baking parchment), cut down to fit the tin.

Add the rice mixture to the prepared tin and lightly press it down. Top with the reserved coconut syrup. Bake for 20–25 minutes until the edges are slightly bubbling.

Remove from oven and leave to cool completely before cutting and serving.

# filipino-style coconut and sesame rice cakes

**Makes**
15

**Prep Time**
30 minutes

50g (¼ cup) caster (superfine) sugar
2 Tbsp toasted sesame seeds
20g (¼ cup) desiccated (unsweetened shredded) coconut
100g (¾ cup) glutinous rice flour, or as needed

These coconut rice cakes are what my mum calls a good dessert – i.e., 'not too sweet'. They are perfect with a cup of tea.

In a bowl, mix together the sugar and sesame seeds. Place the desiccated coconut in a separate bowl. Set both aside.

In a third bowl, mix the glutinous rice flour with 100ml (scant ½ cup) water, then knead by hand for a few minutes until a smooth dough is formed. If the dough is too wet, add an extra teaspoon of glutinous rice flour until you get the desired consistency. Divide the dough into 15 equal pieces, roll into balls, then flatten into discs about 5mm (¼in) thick.

Bring a saucepan of water to the boil, then add the rice cakes, a couple at a time, and cook until they float to the top. This should only take a couple of minutes. Remove with a slotted spoon to a plate.

Toss the cakes into the bowl of desiccated coconut and turn to coat well on both sides.

Finally, sprinkle the cakes with the sugar and sesame seeds and serve. These are best eaten fresh.

# saffron rice pudding

**Serves**
4

**Prep Time**
1 hour 45 minutes

90g (½ cup) raw basmati rice, washed and drained
pinch of salt
200g (1 cup) caster (superfine) sugar, or to taste
2 Tbsp flaked (slivered) almonds
25g (1oz) unsalted butter
⅛ tsp ground saffron mixed with ½ Tbsp water
2 Tbsp rose water

**To decorate**
ground cinnamon
chopped pistachios

**Fragrant and comforting, this is an elevated version of a classic rice pudding.**

Place the rice in a large saucepan and add 800ml (3½ cups) of water and the salt. Bring to a gentle boil while stirring.

Partially cover the pan with a lid and leave to cook over a low heat for about 1 hour, or until the rice is soft and the mixture is thick. Make sure you stir it occasionally.

Add the sugar (you can reduce the amount if you want it less sweet), almonds, butter, saffron water and rose water. Mix until well combined.

Continue cooking for another 30 minutes, or until the rice pudding is creamy and thick. If it is still very liquid, keep cooking it down until it reaches the desired consistency.

Serve in bowls with a sprinkle of cinnamon and pistachios on top.

# crispy rice bars with sea salt

**Makes**
20

**Prep Time**
20 minutes (plus
1 hour chilling)

170g (6oz) unsalted butter
600g (15 cups) mini
    marshmallows
230g (9½ cups) puffed
    rice cereal (such as
    Rice Krispies)
397g (14oz) tin of caramel
300g (10½oz) plain (dark)
    or milk chocolate, melted
sea salt flakes, to decorate

Sweet and salty is one of my favourite combos. This one's a crowd pleaser! It's messy, but in all the best ways.

Line the base and sides of a deep 23 x 33cm (9 x 13in) baking tin with baking parchment.

Gently melt the butter in a very large saucepan over a medium heat, then add the marshmallows and mix until completely melted.

Add the puffed rice cereal and mix until it is fully coated in the buttery marshmallow mixture.

Spread the mixture over the base of the prepared tin, pressing it down lightly with a spatula.

Spread over the caramel and transfer the tin to the refrigerator until the caramel layer has firmed up a little.

Cover with the melted chocolate and sprinkle some sea salt flakes on top.

Leave to set in the fridge before cutting. It will be a bit messy to cut, but it's so so worth it! Store in an airtight container for up to 3 days.

# index

## a

arancini balls 15
arborio rice: cheesy arancini balls 15
  mushroom risotto 127
  prawn and mussel paella 67
  prawn risotto 104
asopao, chicken 119
aubergines (eggplants):
  one-pan Middle Eastern chicken and rice 46
avocados: vegan burrito bowl 107

## b

ban xeo 130
bananas: crispy rice paper banana rolls 167
  puttu 78
basmati rice: black pepper rice 146
  butter chicken biryani 111–12
  carrot and raisin pulao 68
  easy tahdig 151
  ghee rice 137
  golden turmeric rice 149
  Indian rice pudding brûlée 164
  lamb kabsa 113–14
  lamb Kabuli pulao 94
  no-fail white rice 134
  one-pan Middle Eastern chicken and rice 46
  one-pan peri peri chicken and rice 61
  saffron rice pudding 179

south Indian lemon rice 142
south Indian yoghurt rice 63
spicy rice and peas 155
Sri Lankan coconut rice with sambal 116
the ultimate chicken biryani 90–1
beans: spicy rice and peas 155
  vegan burrito bowl 107
beansprouts: ban xeo 130
  veggie bibimbap 99
beef: beef pepper rice 51
  loco moco 100
  one-pot chilli beef rice 75
bell peppers *see* peppers
bibimbap, veggie 99
biryani: butter chicken biryani 111–12
  the ultimate chicken biryani 90–1
black beans: vegan burrito bowl 107
black pepper rice 146
bread: rice flour rotis 86
broken rice with lemongrass pork chops 122
broth, herby chicken bone 108
brown butter and miso crispy rice treats 170
brownies, chewy mochi 169
burrito bowl, vegan 107
butter: butter chicken biryani 111–12
  garlic butter rice 138

## c

cabbage: rice flour veggie pakoras 37
  veggie rice paper dumplings 19
Cajun spice 11
cakes: chewy mochi brownies 169
caramel: crispy rice bars with sea salt 180
  Indian rice pudding brûlée 164
carrots: carrot and raisin pulao 68
  fresh rice paper summer rolls 84
  herby chicken bone broth 108
  lamb Kabuli pulao 94
  quick and easy veg fried rice 48
  veggie bibimbap 99
  veggie rice paper dumplings 19
cashew nuts: black pepper rice 146
cauliflower: harissa-roasted cauliflower and rice salad 71
chaat, puffed rice 20
cheat's mango sticky rice 161
cheese: cheesy arancini balls 15
  cheesy fried sesame balls 42
  mushroom risotto 127
  prawn risotto 104
  red rice and pomegranate salad 59

**182**
index

chewy mochi brownies 169
chicken: butter chicken biryani 111–12
  chicken asopao 119
  crispy rice-coated chicken strips 30
  easy roast chicken pho 80
  Greek-style chicken, rice and lemon soup 97
  herby chicken bone broth 108
  nasi goreng 102
  one-pan Middle Eastern chicken and rice 46
  one-pan peri peri chicken and rice 61
  the ultimate chicken biryani 90–1
chilli oil egg-fried rice 144
chillies: butter chicken biryani 111–12
  dipping sauce 122, 130
  herby chicken bone broth 108
  herby pork and green bean rice bowl 57
  one-pot chilli beef rice 75
  rice cutlets 29
  rice flour veggie pakoras 37
  south Indian lemon rice 142
  south Indian yoghurt rice 63
  Thai-style basil fried rice 72
  the ultimate chicken biryani 90–1
  vegan tomato rice 54

chocolate: chewy mochi brownies 169
  chocolate and peanut butter crispy rice bites 173
  crispy rice bars with sea salt 180
  crispy rice paper banana rolls with chocolate dip 167
cilantro *see* coriander
coconut: coconut sambal 116
  Filipino-style coconut and sesame rice cakes 176
  puttu 78
  Sri Lankan coconut rice with sambal 116
coconut milk 11
  cheat's mango sticky rice 161
  Filipino-style sticky rice cake 174
  fragrant coconut rice 148
  spicy rice and peas 155
condensed milk: Indian rice pudding brûlée 164
  rice pudding ice lollies 162
cooking tips 8–9
coriander (cilantro): coriander and lime rice 140
  south Indian lemon rice 142
corn kernels see sweetcorn
courgettes (zucchini): veggie bibimbap 99
crackers, crispy rice paper 24
cream: strawberry cream mochi 159
crispy rice bars with sea salt 180

crispy rice bites with imitation crab 17
crispy rice-coated chicken strips 30
crispy rice paper banana rolls 167
crispy rice paper crackers 24
crispy rice salad 27
cucumber: crispy rice salad 27
  Mediterranean tofu rice bowls 52
curry: butter chicken biryani 111–12
  lamb Kabuli pulao 94
  rice cutlets 29
  the ultimate chicken biryani 90–1
curry leaves: black pepper rice 146
  idli 128
  south Indian lemon rice 142
  Sri Lankan coconut rice 116
  vegan tomato rice 54
cutlets, rice 29

## d

dates: chocolate and peanut butter crispy rice bites 173
dipping sauce 19, 122, 130
dosas 125
dumplings, veggie rice paper 19

**e**

edamame: crispy rice salad 27
eggplants *see* aubergines
eggs: chilli oil egg-fried rice 144
  loco moco 100
  quick and easy veg fried rice 48
  Spam, eggs and rice 64
evaporated milk: rice pudding ice lollies 162

**f**

Filipino-style coconut and sesame rice cakes 176
Filipino-style sticky rice cake 174
fish sauce: dipping sauce 130
fragrant coconut rice 148

**g**

garam masala 11
garlic: garlic butter rice 138
  ten-minute garlic rice noodles 83
ghee 11
  ghee rice 137
glutinous (sticky) rice 8
  cheat's mango sticky rice 161
  chewy mochi brownies 169
  Filipino-style coconut and sesame rice cakes 176
  Filipino-style sticky rice cake 174
  strawberry cream mochi 159
gochujang: spicy rice cake and sausage skewers 23
  tteokbokki 76
golden turmeric rice 149
Greek-style chicken, rice and lemon soup 97
green beans: herby pork and green bean rice bowl 57
ground spices 10

**h**

harissa-roasted cauliflower and rice salad 71
herbs 11
hot sauces 11

**i**

ice lollies, rice pudding 162
idli 128
Indian rice pudding brûlée 164
ingredients 10–11

**j**

Japanese short-grain rice 8
jasmine rice: broken rice 122
  coriander and lime rice 140
  fragrant coconut rice 148
  garlic butter rice 138
  herby pork and green bean rice bowl 57
  loco moco 100
  nasi goreng 102
  Thai-style basil fried rice 72
jerk spice 11

**k**

kabsa, lamb 113–14
kimbap, mini veggie 32
kimchi rice balls 35

**l**

lamb: lamb kabsa 113–14
  lamb Kabuli pulao 94
Lebanese 7 spice 11
lemon: Greek-style chicken, rice and lemon soup 97
  south Indian lemon rice 142
lemongrass pork chops 122
lentils 11
lime: coriander and lime rice 140
  dipping sauce 122, 130
loco moco 100
lollies, rice pudding 162
long-grain rice 8
  broken rice 122
  chicken asopao 119
  crispy rice dosas 125
  Greek-style chicken, rice and lemon soup 97
  harissa-roasted cauliflower and rice salad 71
  Mediterranean tofu rice bowls 52
  Mexican-style spicy rice 140

one-pot chilli beef rice 75
rice pudding ice lollies 162
south Indian yoghurt rice 63
Turkish rice with vermicelli 153
vegan tomato rice 54

## m

mangoes: cheat's mango sticky rice 161
marshmallows: brown butter and miso crispy rice treats 170
   crispy rice bars with sea salt 180
Mediterranean tofu rice bowls 52
medium-grain rice 8
Mexican-style spicy rice 140
microwave rice 8
Middle Eastern chicken and rice 46
milk: chewy mochi brownies 169
   Indian rice pudding brûlée 164
   rice pudding ice lollies 162
mini veggie kimbap 32
miso: brown butter and miso crispy rice treats 170
mochi: chewy mochi brownies 169
   strawberry cream mochi 159
mushrooms: cheesy arancini balls 15
   loco moco 100
   mushroom risotto 127

veggie bibimbap 99
veggie rice paper dumplings 19
mussels: prawn and mussel paella 67

## n

nasi goreng 102
no-fail white rice 134
noodles: easy roast chicken pho 80
   ten-minute garlic rice noodles 83
   Turkish rice with vermicelli 153
nori: mini veggie kimbap 32
   spicy tuna onigiri 38

## o

one-pan Middle Eastern chicken and rice 46
one-pan peri peri chicken and rice 61
one-pot chilli beef rice 75
onigiri, spicy tuna 38
onions: butter chicken biryani 111–12

## p

paella, prawn and mussel 67
pakoras, rice flour veggie 37
pancakes: ban xeo 130
   crispy rice dosas 125
peanut butter: chocolate and peanut butter crispy rice bites 173
peanuts: puffed rice chaat 20

south Indian lemon rice 142
peppercorns: black pepper rice 146
peppers (bell): chicken asopao 119
   one-pot chilli beef rice 75
   prawn and mussel paella 67
   sofrito 119
   vegan burrito bowl 107
peri peri chicken and rice 61
pho, easy roast chicken 80
'pizza', Vietnamese rice paper 40
pomegranate seeds: red rice and pomegranate salad 59
pork: braised pork belly rice 121
   broken rice with lemongrass pork chops 122
   herby pork and green bean rice bowl 57
potatoes: rice flour veggie pakoras 37
prawns (shrimp): ban xeo 130
   prawn and mussel paella 67
   prawn risotto 104
   Thai-style basil fried rice 72
puffed rice: brown butter and miso crispy rice treats 170
   chocolate and peanut butter crispy rice bites 173
   crispy rice bars with sea salt 180

crispy rice-coated chicken strips 30
puffed rice chaat 20
pulao: carrot and raisin pulao 68
lamb Kabuli pulao 94
puttu 78

## q
quick and easy veg fried rice 48

## r
raisins: carrot and raisin pulao 68
lamb Kabuli pulao 94
ready-cooked rice 8
red kidney beans: spicy rice and peas 155
red rice and pomegranate salad 59
reheating rice 10
rice cakes: Filipino-style coconut and sesame rice cakes 176
idli 128
spicy rice cake and sausage skewers 23
tteokbokki 76
rice cookers 8
rice cutlets 29
rice flour 10
ban xeo 130
cheesy fried sesame balls 42

puttu 78
rice flour rotis 86
rice flour veggie pakoras 37
rice paper: crispy rice paper banana rolls 167
crispy rice paper crackers 24
fresh rice paper summer rolls 84
veggie rice paper dumplings 19
Vietnamese rice paper 'pizza' 40
rice pudding ice lollies 162
risotto: mushroom risotto 127
prawn risotto 104
rotis, rice flour 86

## s
saffron rice pudding 179
salads: crispy rice salad with tahini and lemon 27
harissa-roasted cauliflower and rice salad 71
red rice and pomegranate salad 59
sambal, coconut 116
sauce, dipping 19, 122, 130
sausages: spicy rice cake and sausage skewers 23
scallions see spring onions
seafood sticks: crispy rice bites with imitation crab 17

sesame seeds: cheesy fried sesame balls 42
Filipino-style coconut and sesame rice cakes 176
sev: puffed rice chaat 20
short-grain rice 8
beef pepper rice 51
braised pork belly rice 121
herby chicken bone broth with rice 108
kimchi rice balls 35
mini veggie kimbap 32
quick and easy veg fried rice 48
spicy tuna onigiri 38
shrimp see prawns
skewers, spicy rice cake and sausage 23
sofrito 119
soups: chicken asopao 119
Greek-style chicken, rice and lemon soup 97
south Indian lemon rice 142
south Indian yoghurt rice 63
soy sauce: dipping sauce 19
Spam, eggs and rice 64
spice mixes 11
spices 10–11
spicy rice cake and sausage skewers 23
spicy rice and peas 155
spicy tuna onigiri 38
spinach: mini veggie kimbap 32
spring onions (scallions): red rice and pomegranate salad 59

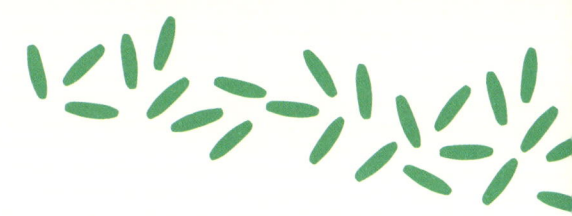

veggie rice paper dumplings 19
Sri Lankan coconut rice 116
storing rice 10
strawberry cream mochi 159
summer rolls 84
sushi rice 8
   chilli oil egg-fried rice 144
   crispy rice bites with imitation crab 17
   Spam, eggs and rice 64
   veggie bibimbap 99
sweetcorn (corn) kernels:
   beef pepper rice 51
   vegan burrito bowl 107
   Vietnamese rice paper 'pizza' 40

## t

tahdig 151
tahini, crispy rice salad with 27
ten-minute garlic rice noodles 83
Thai-style basil fried rice 72
tofu: Mediterranean tofu rice bowls 52
   veggie rice paper dumplings 19
tomatoes: chicken asopao 119

vegan tomato rice 54
tteokbokki 76
tuna: spicy tuna onigiri 38
Turkish rice with vermicelli 153
turmeric: golden turmeric rice 149

## U

the ultimate chicken biryani 90–1
urad dal: crispy rice dosas 125

## V

vegan burrito bowl 107
vegan tomato rice 54
veggie bibimbap 99
veggie rice paper dumplings 19
vermicelli, Turkish rice with 153
Vietnamese rice paper 'pizza' 40

## y

yoghurt rice, south Indian 63

## z

za'atar 11
zucchini see courgettes

# about the author

Rene Subash is a passionate self-taught home cook and content creator, born in Bangalore, India, now living in Liverpool, UK, with her family. Whilst working as a nurse through the COVID-19 pandemic, Rene started sharing her recipes online as a way of getting her mind off stressful days at work and @Renes.Cravings was born. Since then, she has amassed an engaged TikTok and Instagram following through showcasing global recipes with high energy, lots of personality and fun!

# acknowledgements

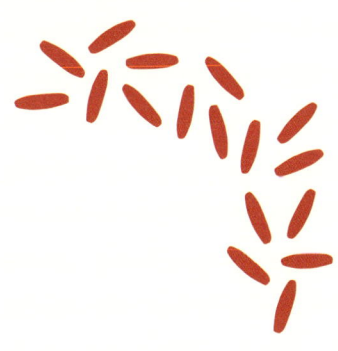

I owe a huge thank you to my family, my parents who supported me along the journey, my little sister who was never afraid to give me her honest opinions on my recipes, and my grandma. Or Ammechi as I like to call her in Malayalam. Her love for cooking has always inspired me and I will forever be grateful to her for sharing her incredible recipes with me.

Thank you to all of the people who have helped me along the way and to the incredible team that made this book into a reality – thanks for being so patient with me and my ideas throughout the process.

And lastly, a huge thank you to my followers. The support you have given @Renes.Cravings is the reason why I am able to even have the opportunity to write this book. None of it goes unnoticed.

Thank you always x

Quadrille, Penguin Random House UK,
One Embassy Gardens, 8 Viaduct Gardens,
London SW11 7BW

Quadrille Publishing Limited is part of the Penguin Random House group of companies whose addresses can be found at global.penguinrandomhouse.com

Copyright © Quadrille 2025
Photography © Haarala Hamilton 2025
Design © Quadrille 2025

Penguin Random House values and supports copyright. Copyright fuels creativity, encourages diverse voices, promotes freedom of expression and supports a vibrant culture. Thank you for purchasing an authorized edition of this book and for respecting intellectual property laws by not reproducing, scanning or distributing any part of it by any means without permission. You are supporting authors and enabling Penguin Random House to continue to publish books for everyone. No part of this book may be used or reproduced in any manner for the purpose of training artificial intelligence technologies or systems. In accordance with Article 4(3) of the DSM Directive 2019/790, Penguin Random House expressly reserves this work from the text and data mining exception.

Published by Quadrille in 2025

www.penguin.co.uk

A CIP catalogue record for this book is available from the British Library

ISBN 9781837833429
10 9 8 7 6 5 4 3 2 1

Colour reproduction by F1

Printed in China by C&C Offset Printing Co., Ltd.

The authorised representative in the EEA is Penguin Random House Ireland, Morrison Chambers, 32 Nassau Street, Dublin D02 YH68.

Penguin Random House is committed to a sustainable future for our business, our readers and our planet. This book is made from Forest Stewardship Council® certified paper.

**Managing Director, Publishing**
Sarah Lavelle

**Editorial Director**
Sophie Allen

**Assistant Editor**
Ellie Spence

**Designer**
Katy Everett

**Photographer**
Haarala Hamilton

**Food Stylist**
El Kemp

**Food Stylist Assistants**
Aine Pretty-McGrath and Georgia Rudd

**Prop Stylist**
Rachel Vere

**Head of Production**
Stephen Lang

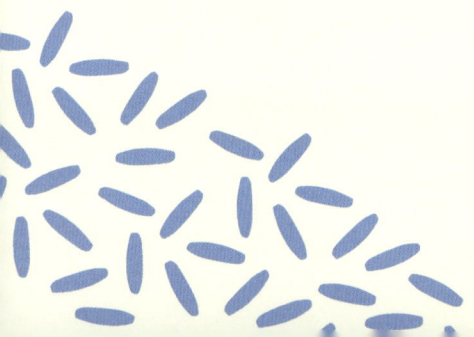